COMMUNICATING WITH KIDS
A Practical Guide to the Forgotten Language

Best Wishes
Gabo Lockhart

COMMUNICATING WITH KIDS
A Practical Guide to the Forgotten Language

by Estes J. Lockhart, Ed.D.

Undercurrents Press
Frederick, Maryland

All names of clients used in this book are fictitious.

FIRST EDITION

Library of Congress Catalog Card No. 89-051053

ISBN 0-9623538-0-9 (paperback edn.)
ISBN O-9623538-2-5 (hardcover edn.)

**TO SALLY, MY WIFE
FOR BELIEVING AND LOVING**

ACKNOWLEDGEMENTS

A number of teachers, colleagues and friends have contributed to this work.

Jay Haley taught me family therapy, and Susan Walen taught me cognitive behavioral therapy. While what I do is not a precise rendering of their work, not a day passes that I don't use something I learned from them.

Richard Wiseman taught me the transformational power of language, and though he would deny it, I feel certain he is Magister Ludi.

Dale Depweg was my first companion on the metaphor journey.

I want to thank two dear old friends, Ken Burlingame and Larry Harper. Both have contributed to this book in more ways than words can tell.

Colleagues who contributed analogies for this work and clients who used the analogies, images and metaphors to grow deserve thanks.

In addition I am grateful to Kim Roberts, Robert Muse, B.J. Muse and Marion Root for manuscript assistance, Russell Beaton for editing and Sally Lockhart for the final editing.

FOREWORD

This book is based on my work with kids, their teachers and their parents. It is addressed primarily to counselors and parents, but will also be useful to teachers, school administrators, and those in agencies which seek to help kids. In writing this book, I have drawn on my personal experiences in the role of teacher, school counselor, clinical mental health counselor in private practice, school principal, parent and kid.

Throughout my work, I searched for a book which would give me the keys to open doors to deeper levels of communication with kids. Never finding such a book, I have written this one. It is a straightforward account of what I have found to be most useful in connecting with kids.

This book is about the power that can be found in everyday language if one knows how to use it. For example, when a kid says he doesn't know if he has the strength to carry through on a task, instead of saying, "Sure you do!," one can say, "We're like teabags. We don't know how strong we are till we get into hot water." This grabs a kid's attention, because it gives him something he wasn't expecting -- an unusual twist on an image from everyday life that applies directly to him. And it's safe. It doesn't put him on the spot by saying he can do something that he doubts he can do. It's an image that simply says, when things get tough, we can be stronger than we expect. You don't need to be a poet to say these things, but you do need to have a storehouse of them. I've recorded in this book hundreds of these vivid images -- and strategies for using them. I've included an index to the analogies by presenting problem and an extensive bibliography for those who wish to further explore the techniques.

This book points the way to the creative use of everyday language for the crucial task of helping our kids. For a start, it can be used as a practical guide to what to say. But my hope is that the reader will go beyond using it cookbook fashion. My hope is that the reader will become a metaphor enthusiast, always keeping a sharp eye and ear for the analogy or story that, like a fine piece of art, communicates on a deeper level.

Estes Lockhart
Frederick, 1989

TABLE OF CONTENTS

"I *am* listening, Dad.
You're just not saying
the right thing."

Innes Lockhart
8 years old

THE SAME OLD PROBLEM

"Our earth is degenerate...Children no longer obey their parents."

Egyptian Priest 4000 B.C.

"Our youth love luxury. They have bad manners, contempt for authority, disrespect for older people. Children nowadays are tyrants. They no longer rise when their elders enter the room. They contradict their parents, chatter before company, gobble their food, and tyrannize their teachers."

Socrates 399 B.C.

"Our young men have grown slothful. Their talents are left idle, and there is not a single honorable occupation for which they will toil day and night. Slumber and languor, have entered into mens' hearts... Without strength, without energy, they add nothing during life to the gifts with which they are born, and they complain of their lot."

Senecca 100 A.D.

"I would there were no age between ten and three-and-twenty, or that youth would sleep out the rest; for there is nothing in the between but getting wenches with child, wronging the ancientry, stealing, and fighting."

Shakespeare 1623 A.D.

"I urge all federal, state and local officials to assist...in the restoration of discipline."

Ronald Reagan 1984

1

TOUCHING BASE

*"The difference between the right word and
the almost right word is the difference
between lightning and the lightning bug."*

Mark Twain

**KIDS CAN SLIP PAST US WHILE WE STRUGGLE
TO REACH THEM.**
How do you reach them?
What do you say to kids?
How can you communicate at deeper levels?
HOW DO SUCCESSFUL THERAPISTS DO IT?
Therapists know kids are in too big a rush to listen.
Kids have got exciting things to do. Therapists often grab
kids' attention with brief analogies, stories, images and
other communication strategies. For example if a kid says
he is floundering trying to get his project done, stay in
school, cope with his parent's divorce, or a peer's
rejection, a counselor might say,

Hang in there, it's pressure that makes diamonds.

It's a simple statement but it can be the lifeline a kid
needs to stay afloat in a time of stress.

PLAYING ZEN GAMES

Using brief sayings to reach kids is in the teaching spirit of the Zen masters. Zen teaches not by lecture but by directly pointing to what is obvious. As Suzuki said, *"Zen is like looking for the glasses that sit on our nose."* Reaching kids by using analogies, and images that point to the obvious can be powerful because it allows kids to have an "ah ha" experience or at least to gain insight on their own.

SEEKING HELP FROM OTHERS

This book provides images which encourage kids to drop their defenses and seek the help of others. The more the kid succeeds by being open to suggestions from others, the better he will get along in life. A good way to put it for kids is:

All great athletes can far out perform
their coaches but they wouldn't think
of going into competition without one.

Learning to seek another's perspective can make all the difference in life. My own favorite image of this openness to another's perspective is that of Albert Einstein who on his death bed was reading the work of Velikovsky, a Russian scientist, who strongly argued against Einstein's own theory of gravity.

THINKING BEFORE ACTING

This book provides hundreds of analogies, images and strategies for helping kids' think before they act. Some problems addressed are: motivation, parenting, family problems, identity, school achievement, anger, loss, disrespect, fighting, depression, divorce, change, attention seeking, peer relations, self esteem, anxiety. crisis coping, delinquency, cults, decision making.

CONNECTING WITH KIDS

This book shows how the author connected with real **kids in counseling.** Some of the kids described have more serious problems than the average family has to confront. By looking at extreme problems we are able to see the basic underlying dynamics of the "average" kid's difficulty more clearly.

MAKING THE MESSAGE STICK

This book is packed with lists of nuts and bolts **suggestions for encouraging kids to value and use** **analogies.** Highly successful counselors don't just throw out some images and analogies for the kid to think about. They don't just say, "let me tell you about something that once happened to me," and let it go at that. Counselors use a wide range of strategies to eke out every bit of mileage from each image and analogy. **This book is** **packed with practical suggestions on:**

How to prevent resistance and opposition.

Do's and don't's of productive discussions.

How to help a kid out of a crisis.

How to improve family communication.

How to help a kid succeed in school.

How to help a kid through the rites of passage.

These strategies and guidelines are described in depth and illustrated with case histories of real kids. The strategies help you to use the analogy or image in a way that appeals to kids.

GRABBING AND HOLDING THE KID'S INTEREST

The broad range of communication skills that counselors use to hold kids' attention are described in this book so as to make them accessible to anyone.

This book is unique because of its focus on the practical use of brief analogy and image. To my knowledge this is the first time that this many analogies and images along with detailed instructions for using them in the context of a kid's problem has been published. Whether we are counselors, teachers or parents, we soon learn,

> **We can lecture the average kid**
> **until we are blue in the face and**
> **get nowhere! On the other hand say,**
> **"Listen to what happened to me!"**

At least for a moment, most kids will look around with interest when someone begins to tell a story. Lest the moment escape, we need to have an interesting short statement that will make the kid wonder about positive ways to address his troubles without evoking resistance and opposition. Analogies can do this.

CONFRONTING A KID WITH STORIES

If you have been trying to help an adolescent who curses, fights, withdraws or throws tantrums because he thinks everyone treats him unfairly, you won't get very far telling him that the world is unfair, and he just needs to learn how to deal with it. A better way is to use analogical questioning by asking the kid,

> *If you were swimming at the beach*
> *and you found yourself being pulled*
> *under and out to sea by a powerful*
> *current under the water. What would*
> *you do?*

This is an interesting dilemma that resembles the kid's problem. It is certainly unfair for an undertow to pull the kid out to sea under the water. It attracts the kid's curiosity because it is a matter of life and death. In case a kid seems uninterested by the analogy, I usually add, "Well, if you're ever in that situation, remember, as you are gasping for your last breath, that you could have learned how to save your life from this old, gray bearded guy."

Most kids then respond, if only to find out what they are supposed to do to save their life. I then let the kid struggle on his own with the dilemma. The way a smart swimmer would solve the problem would be to go with the current and swim slowly to the side and out of it. The solution to being caught in an undertow is the same as the solution to being treated unfairly in life. The kid needs to learn how to accept reality and flow with it rather than fight it. This allows him some control over his life, a way out of being destroyed by powers, no matter how unfair, that are stronger than he.

TAKING ANOTHER PERSPECTIVE

An analogy helps the kid to consider his situation from another perspective. Viewing the problem from a third person perspective reduces resistance and opposition. Learning to see one's problems as well as the problems of others from a third person perspective is often a weak ability in children exhibiting maladaptive behaviors (Urbain & Kendall,1980). Piaget(1926) said that all kids begin life ignorant of the feelings of others, mature in part through stages of acquiring social perspective taking skills by interaction with peers and others socially.

The kid who has difficulty interacting with others, loses the chance to learn perspective taking. Without perspective taking, he has difficulty interacting with others. It's a vicious cycle. The skillful use of analogy can get around the fear of failure cycle that makes kids with weak social skills defensive and unwilling to even try to learn. For example if a kid says, "I've never won at any thing, and I'm never going to," a powerful eye opener for him can be to say,

You may not realize it but you have actually
won one of the greatest struggles in life." and
when he looks in wonder and disbelief you can tell
him "You were in a race with 150 to 600 million sperm
to fuse with an egg and initiate your life,
and you won the first great race of all and are alive.

RESISTING PEER PRESSURE WITH ANALOGIES

The pressure to follow a friend's irresponsible lead in order to be accepted is a danger for kids. When friends invite a kid to do something fun with them, a kid may say yes without thinking it through unless some association or image of warning pops into the kid's head. For example, a kid may quickly follow his friends into a river to play not thinking of swift undercurrents that could end his life suddenly. How much safer if when the kid came to the unknown, be it river or otherwise, he associated opportunities for fun with the possibility of danger. It can be crucial for a kid to have analogies, images and stories which guide his decision making.

ENLISTING HELP FROM THE UNCONSCIOUS

Analogies work at the unconscious as well as conscious levels to help resolve problems. This is exemplified well in statements of scientists who recount making discoveries by relating images from their dreams to their scientific work. Kekule Von Stradonitz is credited with having laid the ground work for the modern structural theory of organic chemistry by a discovery which was made through an image in a dream. One night in 1865 *Kekule dreamed of the benzene molecule as a snake whirling round and round biting its tail.* Using that image as an analogy his concept of the six carbon benzene ring was born and the facts of organic chemistry known up to that time fell into place.

Similarly, I had a kid named Jamie come in and tell me a weird dream in which he was trying to stop a bunch of hoods from selling drugs to young children. To make a long story short, Jamie told me he decided that he was being duped like the little kids, but the game was over. Jamie said, "No more drugs for me."

While on a conscious level Jamie had been arguing that drugs weren't a problem, on an unconscious level he was questioning how wise it was to continue using drugs. Jamie's case points out how analogies and images can enlist the power of the unconscious in the service of positive behavior change in a kid.

Analogies that come from dreams are a rare and special occurrence. That is why we must give kids images and brief analogies.

SAVING FACE WHEN CHANGING

In the example above, Jamie also saved face. He took the advice he found in a dream rather than the advice that adults had been giving. It made the decision to act his decision. This finding of a way to save face while changing is especially important for many an adolescent who is desperately attempting to gain power, independence and a sense of identity.

BREAKING THROUGH ASSUMPTIONS WITH HUMOR

Sometimes a kid's biggest problem is that he has made some assumption which he arrogantly hangs on to despite the fact that it causes him trouble. No one, especially a child or adolescent, likes to be told his belief is wrong. For example a kid might tell you that disobeying his parents, smoking marijuana or driving fast in cars isn't going to hurt him. It might be impossible to get him to even consider the evidence against his assumption. I shudder now to remember on saturday mornings sneaking over to an abandoned stock car track and racing junkers with my teenage friends. If my more mature self could travel back in time and try to get us kids to listen to reason, I know it wouldn't have slowed us down one bit. On the other hand we might have listened to a dramatic story.

Oswald Spengler in his classic *The Decline of the West* wrote that "We use mathematics to understand dead forms and analogy to understanding living forms." Kids will store away an interesting story or thought and later use it as an analogy to understand and help resolve a problem of their own. One of the first things to do with a kid who knows it all is to get him to see that all of us are capable of looking foolish if we decide that we know it all and begin making unfounded assumptions without checking them out. A humorous analogy to help kids understand how easy it is for us all to make unfounded assumptions is the story of the "The Captain in the fog." It goes like this:

The captain of a ship noticed light directly ahead on a night filled with dense fog. He quickly flashed a signal for the other boat to give way. Almost immediately the response he got was for him to give way. He then flashed a message that he was an admiral in the navy. The message shot back to him was that the sender was a mere seaman but that nevertheless the captain had better turn around as quickly as possible. The captain, now very frustrated, and angry sent a message stating that he was on the largest battleship afloat. The message he received back through the fog was, "I am on a lighthouse!"

A story such as this one is not going to immediately make a kid who thinks he knows it all start acting humble. It is one more experience for him to build on in attempting to find a way out of his purely self-centered perspective. Also, every time the kid decides to tell the story to a friend or just think about an analogy that struck him as interesting, he is instructing himself in a new way of thinking and viewing the world around him. With increasing age kids are able to control behavior more by following self instructions than by following the instructions of adults (Luria, 1961). Analogies give kids some material to use in restructuring the way they think and act.

BUILDING & REBUILDING FAMILY RELATIONSHIPS

No matter what the problems a family brings to me, they usually require the building or strengthening of a relationship. Everyone would like to solve his problem instantly, and so one of the first things he must realize is that Rome wasn't built in a day. Most serious problems have too many facets to be taken on all at once. They have to be worked on bit by bit with consistency, persistence and creative problem solving.   If you try to rebuild a broken relationship in a day, you're just as likely to drive the kid father away! Think about how you feel when anyone tries to come on to you too quickly, particularly if for some reason you aren't in the mood for interacting with the person. Even the greatest therapists would agree that rarely do they find simple solutions to complex problems.

Listed below are some opening exclamations of clients during their first counseling session with me.   As you read their crises, ask yourself if they sound like problems that could be fixed instantly?

This is how we sound when we're stuck in the problem with our kid.

COPING WITH CRISES IN HEALTHY FAMILIES

* *"My kid is growing up and we just don't have the close kind of relationship I'd hoped for."*

* *"Our daughter is tremendous, but a couple of rejections from boy friends have got her depressed,not doing her school work and cut off from her family and friends. Nothing we say seems to help."*

* *"My kid tells me she'll be so happy when she can finally leave home. I give her all the love I can."*

* *"My kid refuses to ask me for help on anything. So I never know when homework is due until the last minute, when I see the kid in a panic and force an answer from him."*

* *"My kid just doesn't have a sense of reality. He thinks the world owes him a living."*

* *"My daughter is a time bomb about to blow, and I'm scared I might do or say the wrong thing. I don't want to cause her to try suicide or something."*

* *"If I could just get some support from my husband, I think the children could be managed. But he adds pressure because he is still a child himself."*

* *"My son just refuses to work up to his ability. Counseling hasn't worked. I don't have a clue."*

* *"My daughter tells lies that get her into trouble and embarrass the whole family. There's no reason for her to do it, but she won't stop. I wonder if she is using drugs."*

* *"My son doesn't obey us, and I can see him going right down the terrible road I did."*

Talented counselors can't do anything to instantly solve the crises listed above. Why should parents expect to be able to do so? The first step is to slowly but surely inch by inch build a better relationship. Communication is crucial in building relationships. The analogies and strategies in this book are powerful aides in this process.

CONCLUSION:

Since the beginning of time man has used stories as analogies to his own situation. Analogies have helped him gain self confidence and control over his environment by allowing him to fantasize himself as a hero able to subdue the dangerous forces that assault him. The little kid who plays at being **Superman** is following the same urge to gain a feeling of mastery through fantasy. Viewing *Star Wars*, kids can identify with **Luke Skywalker** who is being trained by a wise spirit to get in touch with the force within himself so that he can become a powerful Jedi Warrior and defeat the evil force in the universe that is attempting destroy humanity.

Even as adults we go to movies such as Steven Spielberg's *Batteries Not Included* to identify with a seemingly impossible situation, where small saucers from outer space save an aging family and their poor young neighbors who are fighting to keep a ruthless and powerful industrialist from tearing down the old building in which they all live.

From the very earliest stories that we read to young children, the pattern emerges of the unconscious working to weave fantasies around what he encounter in reality to give the kid a sense of well being. For example the story of *Cinderella* offers kids an opportunity to learn that crime does not pay and that even though life may treat one unfairly, there is hope. While hearing *Jack And The Beanstalk* and *Snow White*, children can fantasize about a time when they will succeed against the difficult forces of life through there own independent efforts. The poet Schiller said, "Deeper meaning lies in the fairy tales told to me in my childhood than in the truth that is taught by life." Similarly, Charles Steinmetz, who worked in

Edison's lab and ran the lab after Edison left, and who brought about many inventions still used by General Electric and other companies said that he read fairy tales because they contained more wisdom than scientific works! (Deal,T. & Kennedy,A., 1988). The first story I remember my mother reading to me was called *The Little Engine That Could.* Later, I delighted in reading it over and over, and while unaware of it at the time, I was internalizing the story's message: that persistence as much as any other quality we can possess helps us to overcome very difficult obstacles. Children's stories teach the importance of creative problem solving. I remember, for example, a story called *Swimmy* written by Leo Lionni which told of a little fish named Swimmy who saved his whole family from a giant hungry tuna by organizing them in a pattern to look like a larger fish than the tuna.

Whatever our age, we use the powers of the imagination not only to entertain but to give a deeper meaning to our lives. One of the truly great examples of the powerful meaning that can be evoked by a brief incident in a popular movie watched by almost every teenager in our time is the scene in *The Empire Strikes Back* when Darth Vader,the personification of evil, reveals that he is really Luke's father and will die if he ceases to be commanded by the evil force in the universe. Then Darth Vader removes the head piece which is his life support system and the means through which the evil force commands and controls Darth Vader. This act ensures Darth Vader's death. Every teenager in America who watches this movie can experience the realization that even the worse of us, exemplified by Darth Vader, is capable of making the decision to change, to turn over a new leaf, to give all he has, his life, to preserve what is best about us, exemplified in Luke, Darth Vader's son.

Almost since the beginning of time man has been listening to stories and using them for entertainment, communication and transformation. This book describes the practical application of using analogies to communicate with those we love most -- our kids.

2

PREVENTING OPPOSITION

"The power is only in the rules of the game."
--M. Selvini-Palazzoli

EVER HAVE THE FEELING WHEN YOU'RE TALKING WITH A KID THAT HE DOESN'T CARE ABOUT FINDING THE BEST WAY TO DO SOMETHING?

He only cares about being right!

Early in adolescence, kids sometimes feel adrift and powerless. They are old enough to want to enjoy adult privileges, but young enough to be under the control of parents and teachers. In this situation, kids often use relationships as battlegrounds for gaining a sense of power. Kids try to get one up on those around them.

The best way for adults to respond is with a verbal judo in which the adult goes one down in a carefully controlled way to dissipate the power struggle while still remaining in charge. This means giving up power you don't need in order to get power you do need.

Talking about power struggles and going one up or one down reminds me of a story called *How Brer Rabbit Met Tar Baby*. It's a perfect analogy for the mess in which a kid often finds himself. He feels bound up with things

17

he dislikes and is separated from what he really wants.

TAR BABY

In the Tar Baby story, all the beasts got together, Brer Wolf, Brer Bear and the rest, to dig a well and plant crops. However, Brer Rabbit wouldn't help.He spent his time playing and then would sneak a drink from the well or swipe things from the garden when everyone was asleep. So, after warning Brer Rabbit to stop and getting nowhere, Brer Wolf decided to catch him. He took some straw and made a model of a baby. Next he smeared it with soft, sticky black tar all over and placed it right beside the well.

Then along comes Brer Rabbit one night to sneak some water and finds the Tar Baby. "How's yo mudder, family and de chilluns?" Brer Rabbit says at first trying to be very nice. But Tar Baby don't move or say nothing. So Brer Rabbit gets real brave and says, "Look here you better get out my way or I'se gwine hit yo with dis paw and knox you silly." But Tar Baby just sit and don't say nothing. So Brer Rabbit he hit Tar Baby a good lick but then Brer Rabbit's paw sticks fast in the tar. "Let me go" he hollers and hits the Tar Baby with his other fist. It sticks tight in the Tar Baby just like the other one. Then Brer Rabbit say, "Let me go, or I gwine kick de stuffins out of yo." Soon both Brer Rabbit's feet are stuck in the Tar Baby. Then Brer Rabbit slams his head in the Tar Baby and he is stuck tight. When the sun comes up, Brer Rabbit begins to shake all over because he sees Brer Wolf. "Seems you is a little stuck up dis morning Brer Rabbit. Did dat Tar Baby catch you trying to steal again?" "Oh, Brer Wolf," says Brer Rabbit, shaking like a leaf, "thow me in de fire, thow me down de well, but whatever you do don't, please don't thow me in de briar patch." Then Brer Wolf he scratches his head and he says, "You wants me to thow you in de fire or de well. But I'se gwine do the wostest thing you don't want me to do. I'se gwine thow you straight in the briar patch."

18

After Brer Wolf had thrown Brer Rabbit in the Briar Patch, Brer Rabbit called out to him laughing all the while. "Thanks for sending me back home. I and all my family was born and raised in de briar patch."

JUST TRYING TO HAVE SOME FUN

All Brer Rabbit wanted to do was live the good life, but it seemed that no matter what he did, he ended up in trouble. He tried to punch his way into power over Tar Baby. This way of trying to get out of trouble just resulted in him getting stuck worse. Kids describe feeling in the same fix as Brer Rabbit. Every time the kid tries to solve a problem, he makes it worse.

The kid who keeps ending up stuck begins to feel hopeless and a failure. Then what began as a small problem can mushroom into a serious problem often without the kid telling anyone how he feels or asking for help.

One of the best ways to ensure that one's kids don't become seriously troubled is to find a way to get them to listen to the common sense and wisdom that comes from years of living.

THE "MAGIC" SPARK

STRETCH: A Case of Physical Aggression - Self Respect Analogy

Let me tell you about a kid and his family that points up how mystifying the whole process of helping a troubled kid can be. We'll call him Stretch. He liked to be called by a nickname to distance himself from his family. Really they were hard working middle class folks who loved their son dearly and couldn't figure out why he was acting out with them or anyone else.

First they thought they were going to solve his problems by having a psychological assessment done to find out why he was refusing to work, cursing teachers and walking out of class. Instead of finding some "deep underlying problem" they learned that he had a high I.Q. score, that he had no apparent neurological problems, that he was angry with his family because he felt they tried to control and dominate him, and that he evidenced numerous indicators of depression. The recommendation was that he needed "intensive counseling" and an "individualized education program."

The parents immediately went to a psychiatrist expecting to get some "intensive counseling" but after a year Stretch continued to have serious difficulties. The family went for "family therapy" which in this case, unfortunately, amounted to the family, Stretch and the doctor just sitting in the room while Stretch lambasted his family and told them how they never understood. The doctor saw his job as that of attempting to clarify for the family the nature and cause of Stretch's concerns. The parents meanwhile left each session feeling exasperated and guilty but not sure what they could do to change things. It seemed to them that they had done some things in the past that were wrong and for which they would always be guilty. In fact Stretch attacked his father for taking too much lip from his boss without standing up to him.

The teachers had heard that Stretch was in therapy and decided to just try to hold on until the doctor could work his magic. But sometimes when they'd try to help Stretch to get his work done, he'd snap back, "Get off my case, your stressing me out."

Finally Stretch got in trouble in the community for hiding in dark alleys and robbing elderly shoppers of their money. He wanted money for drugs. He was sent off to a juvenile detention program. When he returned, he was placed in an alternative public school, but he continued doing the same things that had gotten him in trouble in school and in the community before. Then a young female counselor built a close relationship with Stretch.

WHAT WORKED

One day shortly before a court hearing the young counselor called him into her office and told him, with tears in her eyes,

*It really makes me sad that you don't have any
more respect for yourself than to do what you
are doing.*

Bing-go! It seemed that from the moment the counselor spoke these words Stretch started to change for the better. Why? Lots of people had been doing lots of things to help but seemed to be getting nowhere. Perhaps it was like starting a fire.

*You need kindling; you need logs; but there is no
flame without a spark. Was the counselor the spark?
If so, how did she hit on the right thing to say?*

This is a true story, and the kid has since graduated and is doing well. I've sat and talked with Stretch about his problems. I've asked him what made him act the way he did, and what made him change. He doesn't have any more idea than the rest of us as to why he was doing what he was doing except that he felt like he was just trying to have a good time, and everybody seemed to be on his case trying to stress him out. He felt that even though his thinking was "stupid" at the time, he was trying to control his life as best he could.

Stretch does, however, remember the counselor telling him that she didn't understand him not respecting himself. He says it mattered to him what she thought, because he really liked her. He said, "She only seemed to want to help, not tell me what to do." He credits her and his own desire to finally make something out of himself as the reason for changing. He also talks about there needing to be something good for a kid to look forward to if he is going to change. "She made me feel like I could get a lot of good things out of life," Stretch said.

A young attractive counselor who asked him about his self respect, a desire to make something of himself and the discovery of something to look forward to: is that a formula for success with troubled kids? NO! Absolutely not! It's what worked for Stretch. You could try it with the next hundred kids you meet and get nowhere. What it says is that we shouldn't stop trying to reach kids.

COMPLEXITY OF A KID'S PROBLEMS

The problems of kids are complex problems without simple answers. What you have to take from Stretch's story is the following:

* There is hope.

* The problem can be solved without anyone, including the kid ever having known what the problem was.

* Stress is what is perceived as stress. Stress can result from symbolic associations with earlier life events. For example, if a kid saw his father treated unfairly, then he may re-experience the associated emotion each time he is treated unfairly in even the slightest way.

* Intensive psychotherapy" is often a euphemism for the concept of "he's got serious problems and needs some very unique but as yet undiscovered intervention by someone with the appropriate skills, and it will take a lot of everyone's time.

* Good family therapy is not a third person sitting in the room letting the kid lambast the family or vice versa. In good family therapy all members learn to form more functional relationships.

* Helping a troubled kid to solve his problems is
not a simple direct procedure with a predictable
outcome. There are usually no ready made answers.
Everyone concerned needs to problem solve
collaboratively, and be persistent.

* Kids with problems can come from good families.

* A psychological report, while it may clarify or
address strengths and weaknesses, is not likely to
uncover a "Deep Underlying Problem" which can
then be addressed and the problem vanish.

* The kid's acts in part result from irrational
thinking about how best to control his life.
An irrational act means any act which gets in the
way of the kid's own goal.

* The magic, the spark, is a significant emotional
experience that needs to be created for the unique
needs of the kid.

* It's hard to figure out what's right to say to a
troubled kid, but if someone happens to say the
right thing, it can make all the difference.

* Often the kid lacks a trusting relationship with
any adult.

Analogies and images can be used to reduce a kid's
stress and engage his imagination and sense of wonder in
solving his problem. But we must not lose sight of the
individual context of the kid's problem. For example, if
we were working with a kid who kept looking to the past
and saying that something someone did or something that
happened in the past was the problem, then we might
wisely decide to encourage the kid to think about how to
solve the problem in the present rather than dwell on the
past. The kid might agree but then go right on blaming
his problems on events in the past. If the kid happened to

be sixteen years old and interested in cars to the exclusion of almost everything, then we might reach the kid by asking him:

Would you drive a car forward by looking through the rear window at where you had been?

Whenever we found the kid blaming his problems on the past, we could say, "Driving by the rear window method again?" In other words, not just the content but the way we say it could become a landmark for reference in other discussions. Kids will typically keep doing the same dysfunctional things over and over before they change. It's important to have a way to talk to them that reinforces a more positive way of doing things but doesn't become nagging. You can repeat it almost like an advertizing jingle.

The goal is to create an image that uniquely fits the context of a problem. It is talk that evokes a significant emotional experience for the moment at hand. It is not necessarily original nor profound. It can be found almost anywhere. Christian parables, Zen sayings, family stories and the other great literature of the world are rich sources for locating analogies.

It is often crucial to use other techniques and methods in conjunction with analogies. These may include behavior modification, an individualized educational program, individual, group and family counseling. On the other hand simply using a number of systems of intervention without talking to a kid in such a way that he feels he has made a useful connection is rarely successful.

STATING THE OBVIOUS

To connect with a kid when talking with him, we can create a story that is an emotional situation that fits the context of his problem or tell him a story out of our past that is analogous to his problem. We can simply ask a question or make a statement in an unusual or interesting way that grabs his interest. For example, if a kid says he's going to hurt himself in some way because he's had it, we might remind him that

No amount of pain will ever make you feel better.

This kind of statement impresses itself upon the kid by stating the obvious in a way that is seldom heard. In another context, for another kid, whose feeling that the task he's been assigned is not worth the effort he's putting out, it might be most appropriate to state the often heard remark that

There is no gain without pain.

KEEPING IT SHORT AND FOCUSED

The point is that when speaking to kids, we need to constantly remind ourselves that it is the quality of our response, not the quantity that matters.I have a story from my own career as a parent that I use to remind myself of this. I was once going on a long harangue with my 12 year old about his poor manners. The next day, when the stress was off and we were just talking, he asked

Isn't it bad manners to lecture people for a long time when you are correcting them?

I also remind myself that **what we resist, persists.** I don't want the kid with whom I'm communicating to become so upset with my manner that he begins to reject my message.

STAYING ONE DOWN

Kids often make poor judgments because they are looking for short cuts out of stressful situations or are desperately struggling for a little sense of power or control. Many times a kid realizes as quickly as we the foolishness of his actions, regrets them, and then denies he acted foolishly, hoping that we will just lay off. Of course, it would be foolish strategy to give a kid the message that simply by denial, he can erase his foolish actions and get by in life. But it's also a waste of time and a definite obstacle to a good relationship with a kid to lecture him on a painful mistake he recognizes he has just made. In this regard,

It is important to stay one down when communicating with a kid.

The more insecure and stressed out the kid is, the more one down we should attempt to be. It is far easier to converse with someone about a problem if we do not engage him in a power struggle. Below are concrete ways to go about staying one down when talking with kid. Remember, Brer Wolf was no fool. He very creatively constructed the Tar Baby that Brer Rabbit bound himself up with in the first place. The Tar Baby took no action, said no words and, in effect, from a strong one down position, totally disarmed Brer Rabbit. Below are guidelines for staying one down while using analogies with kids.

WAYS TO STAY ONE DOWN

1) **Don't play the know it all by saying:**
   a) What does your question indicate about you?
   b) Don't you need to figure that out for yourself?

2) **If you become frustrated, uptight or confused, excuse yourself and leave the room perhaps saying you need to go to the bathroom or take care of some detail.** Then go and seek a solution to your own problems. If you become hostile or upset, it will be difficult to keep from becoming defensive yourself which is a poor model for the kid.

3) **Don't take it for granted that anyone understands you.** Kids often agree to things or say they understand just to get someone off their case.

4) **State your opinion as an idea that might be true, not as an immutable law.**

5) **Don't make negative aspects of a person's situation the primary focus of the discussion.**

6) **Never align yourself with a kid against others, such as his friends, teachers, parents.** This is a mistake even when the kid's attack is valid. If you build a relationship around discussions in which the kid attacks others, then when he decides to mend relationships with the other person he will have to worry about it interfering with his relationship with you.

7) **Never accept any guilt for not playing a role assigned to you by the kid.** For example if he wishes to put you in the role of a know-it-all who doesn't really care what he says, don't accept the role. Let him know you don't.

8) **Search hard for an understanding of a kid's thoughts and feelings.** Know that kids rarely present their real problem upon first communicating with anyone. Rather, a kid will present a more comfortable problem to try to

27

test your skill and commitment.

9) **Listen and ask for the kid's solutions before arriving at or stating your own.**

10) **Offer advice when requested but don't take sole responsibility for solving the kid's problem.**

11) **Always attack the problem and not the kid or his friends.** Kids appreciate that adults think differently from them, but they do not accept the idea that any adult, including their parents, has a right to pass moral or ethical judgments about their behavior or their friend's behavior.

12) **Write down things that you agree upon with a kid and give him a copy.** Then when you are talking with him later you won't have to cover the same territory or get into a discussion of what was just said.

13) **Don't interrupt in a discussion.** It gives the impression that you don't care what the kid has to say but are just anxious to tell him what you think.

14) **Don't allow the kid to take you down a blue blazes path.** Stick to the subject by saying something like, "Now what were we talking about anyway?" rather than saying, "You seem to be off the track"

15) **Show respect for the kid and his significant others.** This doesn't mean you agree to things you don't believe in, but it means you don't make an attempt to discredit his friends.

16) **Do not take part in angry arguments.** It models the idea that it is okay to act out angrily.

17) **Think about what your body language is communicating to the kid.** Are you crossing your arms defensively for example?

18) **Don't make reference to other sources beyond the kid's experience as a way of trying to make a point unless it is in the context of actually explaining material in which the kid shows interest.** For example, do not tell him "studies show..." or "everyone knows..."

19) **Let the kid know clearly from the outset what the rules are in communicating with you.**

20) **Never enter into any deals with a kid which restricts your options for taking action.**

21) **Use "I" messages. Say, for example, "I feel upset when my tools aren't put away," rather than saying, "You should put my tools away." It may seem that the message is the same but it isn't.** It's hard for a kid to attack you for simply making a genuine statement about your feelings.

CONCLUSION

Stay one down. This is the first and most sacred rule for having productive talks with kids. Kids often approach communication as a power struggle. Don't engage kids in power struggles. Simply say from a one down position that the rules exist to insure that a particular goal is achieved, and ask if the kid can outline a better way to achieve the goal. If he can, then drop your plan pronto and go with his.

The second rule is to know that a short, simple statement may turn a kid in a positive direction. **Build a repertoire of analogies for quick, creative, engaging responses.** Use analogies to creatively fit the emotional context of a kid's dilemma. For example if a kid should say that a lot of unfair things have been happening to him for a long time, it can help to point out to him that tough experiences can make him stronger and more attractive. He might be told that bones grow back stronger after being broken, and that it is after diamonds have been cut and chipped away at that they are placed in settings.

3

COMMUNICATING WITH KIDS

*"Speak with words that are soft and sweet for
you never know which ones you may have to eat."*
                              Anonymous

WHEN MERELY BEING HIMSELF GETS A KID IN
CONSTANT TROUBLE WITH FAMILY, FRIENDS OR
SOCIETY, HE HAS A PROBLEM.

Some kids will not recognize or acknowledge the
problem. Others will acknowledge the problem but blame
it on others. For example, one bright fourteen year old kid
in therapy with me framed his problem this way:

*I compare my situation to boats.I was a regular
boat and had been doing okay as a regular boat.
Now my parents are trying to use me as an ice breaker
and I am barely floating.In fact, I may have sunk.*

Almost never does a kid say that he has set out to be
problem. Rather, he tells a story about a situation that's
been giving him trouble. While it can be true that someone
is causing him trouble, it is also true that usually he could
improve his situation without hurting himself or others
through acting out.

Sometimes with a kid who is blaming others for what's coming out of him, I give him a lemon and tell him to squeeze it. I ask him if the squeeze being put on the lemon can make anything besides sour juice come out of the lemon? We then talk about what we want inside ourselves.We also talk about what we want to have happen when the squeeze comes.

Thus it is often the case that while the family, community and school attempts to get the student to accept the fact that he has a serious problem, he tries equally hard to get them to see that the problem isn't his. Others attempt to get the kid to change, and he waits for something to change in the family, school or community to relieve his stress. The result is gridlock.

How can you penetrate a wall of denial to talk with a kid about his problems?

BREAKING THROUGH THE WALL OF DENIAL

Nicole: A Case of Self-Injurious Behavior - Clowning Analogy

Nicole was a great example of kid whose family was in gridlock. Nicole was referred by her parents who were at their wits end. The school had brought them in several times to demand that they do something to keep Nicole from hurting her self. Nicole was a very pretty blond haired girl who for no apparent reason would sit in class and carve on her arms with a pencil, pen, knife, or anything she might have at her disposal. Teachers were frightened by thoughts of what might happen next. Other students were also worried. Friends had come in to see the assistant principal in hopes that someone could do something for Nicole before she attempted to harm herself more.

School staff had attempted to get Nicole to disclose what was bothering her. Nicole always said she didn't know. The parents knew that she was depressed, but couldn't get her to talk about it. They were terrified that she was going to attempt suicide and felt powerless to prevent it.

I knew that Nicole was not just going to walk into my office and confide in me, a total stranger, what she had refused to tell others. For that reason, I didn't begin questioning her about her behavior. She wore long sleeves to cover the marks on her arms. I made a point of not focusing attention on her arms.

CUSHIONING AGAINST PAIN

Instead, I asked her to tell me about what good things were happening in her life. As she attempted to tell me the good things, she ended up describing what was bothering her. I call this **the cushion** strategy. It's a situation in which a person begins to feel free to express himself because the subject being discussed is the farthest thing from what's bothering him. He feels cushioned against any intrusion into his secret, painful world. Because Nicole felt comfortable in the knowledge that there was to be no search of her thoughts and feelings underway, she chose to express herself. And, as the Zen teachers say,

If one attempts to express either just the good or the bad, he will sense an incompleteness because the truth always has at least two sides.

As Nicole strove to express her thoughts and feelings, I thought passively about what she was saying, rejecting my own parenting drive to actively guide and lead her. She, out of her own need for completeness of self-expression, began to fill in both sides of her story.

CHECKING THE CRUCIAL FACTORS

As Nicole told her story during several sessions, I

listened carefully for what I call the crucial factors for connecting with kids. They are:

1. **Motivation: What is fun?**
2. **Peers: How do the comings and goings of friends affect the kid?**
3. **Coping style: How does kid handle stress?**
4. **Cognitive style: Is the kid's thinking clear, rational, and sharp or confused or fuzzy?**
5. **Family: How are they being a family?**
6. **Development: What is the kid's social skill ability?**
7. **Fantasy: Who are the characters and what are the stories of the kid's favorite dreams and memories?**
8. **Verbal style: How does kid express himself?**
9. **Heroes: Who are the kid's heroes?**
10. **Communication: What is the best way to have a productive discussion with the kid?**

Listening for the answers to these questions is no easy job. We are apt to want to get to the answers quickly or force our ideas on the kid. We have to be satisfied with not answering some of the crucial questions as well as we'd like or even at all. We need to keep the questions in the back of our mind as we communicate with a kid. We need to remember the story of the *Tortoise and the Hare.*

> **If going slowly eventually gets us where we want to be, it's a lot faster than pushing the kid and getting nowhere.**

In Nicole's case, I first began to get at the problem that was causing her self-injurious behavior by **listening to little off-hand remarks** that seemed to come as an after thought. Nicole would say that her sister was a great tennis player, and she felt she herself could have been good; but her family had come upon harder times and really couldn't give her the training that she needed.

A statement such as this has two sides. One side is a

simple statement of her family's financial situation, and the other is that they found a way to love her sister more, or at least give her more. I began to look for more examples of this theme of inequality between Nicole and her sister. I noticed that she almost always directed the emotional part of any story or expression about her family toward her father. Later, in family sessions, it became clear that Nicole felt less appreciated by her father than she perceived her sister being.

When we dealt with the issue of inequality in the family sessions, the parents were stunned. Of course, they remembered arguments centering on unfairness, but they expected that kind of thing among sisters. They said that they had treated both girls as equally as they could. Nicole saw it very differently.

What the family thinks has been happening may not be the way the kid has been seeing it.

She saw her sister never being reprimanded as sternly as she had been. She saw her sister off at college having a ball; and she, meanwhile, was not being allowed to join an athletic club because the costs were prohibitive. She remembered her father making time for her sister, but later telling her he was too busy in his new job.

The types of inequality Nicole spoke of are common perceptions in families; they seem to evolve out of life circumstances rather than an attempt on anybody's part to be unfair. It is a systems problem in the family that results from complicated alliances of many different family members over many different "small" problems over much time. For example, it may be that in day to day problems, the older sister and dad formed an alliance in arguing with mom about a stressful situation. It may have been that Nicole took mom's side to protect her, and found herself in opposition to her dad, In this situation Nicole may have slowly unconsciously developed a perception that her dad liked her less than her sister.

In fact, it was not a difference in treatment based on who got more or less of the family's time, money or reprimands that was causing Nicole's difficulties. So if the counselor and/or family had attempted to resolve Nicole's self-injurious behavior problem by setting limits or writing contracts to try to make things more obviously equal, it would have been an exercise in frustration. It was Nicole's perception of a sequence in the family that was the problem.

The family came to decide that the unfairness Nicole felt came from the role they had assigned her. Nicole played the role of the buffoon. The father was shocked to learn that it bothered Nicole to be clowned around with, as he put it. He particularly felt that this was a loving and fun way to relate to his daughter. He was floored to find that she personally felt insulted and attacked.

Why hadn't she said something, he asked.

"It just never seemed the right time," was Nicole's response. The family had unknowingly cast their daughter in the role of the fool by clowning around with her in what they thought was a loving way.

I encouraged a discussion about clowns. I pointed out that clowns were originally thought to be ill-bred persons. We then discussed professional clowning. The family concluded that no one would enjoy being a clown full-time as a personality style, but would prefer to do it for profit or fun on one's own schedule.

Nicole's dad was a sensitive man who needed very little discussion to significantly alter his communication style with Nicole. After the session focusing on clowning, Nicole never cut her arms again. She has since graduated from high school and is happy in her work and life. The family used the clowning analogy to think about their situation. The analogy of the clown made it easy for all to see how to change their relationships in the family.

FINDING MOTIVATORS

What motivates a kid to act as he does?
To answer this question, we first need to decide upon a definition of motivation. We often hear people describe a kid as motivated or not motivated, as though the word motivation implies movement toward a positive end. In this way of thinking, if he's motivated, then things are good. In fact, when you speak with a troubled kid, you are as likely to find him motivated toward an end you consider negative as you are to find him motivated in a positive direction.

There is also the idea implied that motivation is a noun, something that you either have or don't have. People casually speak of whether or not someone has motivation. In fact, **motivation is not anything one can possess in isolation.** Motivation is an interaction between a kid and some other person or goal or both. The key word is interaction. A good way to think about motivation with a kid is to see it as a movement to attend and concentrate on something for reasons a kid may not be willing and/or able to communicate. The ways in which a kid interacts with the world within and without himself is often a mystery to him.

In fact, if he tries to honestly explain his reasons for his actions, he may totally miss the mark due to his own misunderstanding. **Kids, like most other people, attempt to concentrate on those tasks that seem to offer them the best chance for success at whatever they desire. Success breeds success.**

For example, I once worked with a young man who did everything that he could to get kicked out of school. He cursed teachers, fought other students, refused to work in class, cut class and smoked where he wasn't supposed to smoke. Yet when anyone spoke with him, he claimed he was trying his best not to get thrown out of school. What you found if you worked closely with him was that he felt that he only did these things occasionally and kept himself under control most of the time.

He felt that in school he acted out because he got

uptight. He said that in school he felt like he had to do something, and anything he did was bound to violate some rule, so what the heck. Also, I found out that he had little phrases he'd picked up that he lived his life by and justified his actions by. For example, he'd say to himself, "Boys will be boys." Also, he'd say, "Guess I just have to learn the hard way." And there was his,

> **I'm not the first person to have trouble and yet turn out fine.**

Kids often have their own way of organizing their world that is very different from what we'd expect on first listening to them. Kids often speak tangentially, indirectly or paradoxically. **The words a kid uses do not necessarily represent what he really thinks or feels.** The frustration families experience in attempting to talk with kids is clear from a common lament heard by anyone who works with the families of troubled kids. They say, **"Why won't he just tell me what is wrong so that I can help him? All he ever says is, 'I don't know."**

The simple truth is that, unbelievable as it may seem to the family, at the time of his trouble the kid may not be able to express his problem. Sidney, was a kid who was very bright but couldn't tell his family what was bothering him.

CHRONIC NONATTENDANCE

Sidney: A Chronic Case of "I Don't Know!" - Tightrope Analogy

Sidney was a "school phobic" whose family kept saying throughout the therapy sessions over and over, "Why won't you just tell us what you are frightened of at school, Sidney?" Sidney would either refuse to answer or tell them, "If you'd just open your eyes, you'd see!"

Sidney's family had been to a mental health clinic where the idea was to listen to what Sidney said needed to be done because otherwise Sidney's young psyche might be permanently damaged, or he might do as he was threatening, kill himself. At the mental health clinic, the first thing Sidney suggested was that the family give him a new bike. So a contract was drawn up in which gradually Sidney would have to go to school more and more in order to get to ride the bike.

Sidney never went to school at all. He would just get up in the morning and ride off to the house of some adult friends who supported him in his idea that he could do just fine without an education.

Next the educators worked with the family to let Sidney be an assistant in an elementary school just down the road from his house. Sidney had been very successful at the school and was now going to middle school, or I should say refusing to go to middle school. Once again Sidney was great. He rushed off bright and early to elementary school and helped keep all the little kids in line. But he refused to go to middle school himself at all.

So that when the family came to me, we had the unique situation of a kid who refused to go to school and yet was going to school every day. In my sessions, Sidney brought up all the old threats, of suicide and running away. The family claimed it was helpless. However, I had the family decide if they thought Sidney's cognitive processes were sharp, and if he was capable of making a rational decision about such things as suicide and running away. I had them decide whether or not they wanted to support Sidney in his behavior at the cost of making him frightened or helpless.

They, in fact, decided the time to do something was now when Sidney was still under their control. They were willing to risk his killing himself, though they didn't for a minute think he would. They decided to make Sidney go to school by whatever means was necessary. They decided to go to the school also to see that he remained there. They had decided to shatter forever a dysfunctional family sequence.

I made a point of meeting frequently with Sidney

during this time in order to help him attempt to integrate what was at odds in his world. As it turned out, he thought it would be hopeless for him to ever relate to most of the other kids, so he just wanted to drop out. When I discovered this, I got him a job in the school counseling office one period a day to enable him to help other kids and see how many other kids had problems.

One day we had a discussion about some of the kids who came to the counseling office against their will.

I said that sometimes people find themselves out on a tightrope, look down, and realize how high up they are. They then get terrified to the point that they panic, freeze, and can't even walk back. If someone didn't reach over and pull him back to safety, the person who had panicked would eventually fall from the wire and die, I said. Later, I said, when the person is over his fear, he might learn to walk the tightrope wire with no trouble at all.

Sidney came to me months later and said, "You pulled me in didn't you?"

JOINING WITH A KID

Through the whole stressful experience for Sidney, I assured him that while I was his family's consultant on how best to keep him in school, I also was his consultant on how best to cope with having to do something that was very tough for him. The term for this bond I formed with Sidney, even while I was supporting the family to put pressure on him to do something he desperately feared, is called joining. Even though he knew I was arming his family against his dysfunctional actions, he also was excited by the prospect of being treated as an equal with me in our personal journey to understand his world and get him through this horror. I joined with his family in a different kind of way, as adults discussing parenting. **Salvador Minuchin has referred to joining as "the glue** that holds the therapeutic system together." I believe that this joining is what allows us to learn about the internal motivation of a kid and to learn what the kid's tangential talk really means. Four factors seem to promote joining:

Joining Factors

1) **Position oneself at a height similar to the kid's and close to him.**

2) **Talk at the kid's level and in his style.**

3) **Invite the kid in subtle ways to take part in a mutual adventure.**

4) **Convey a sense of being comfortably in control of life and filled with wonder about the unpredictability of things.**

It has now been ten years since I worked with Sidney, and when I see him in town, he still looks at me with those eyes yearning for an adventure. I find myself wanting to get back into the internal world of Sidney, find out what's motivating him. **Exploring the subtleties of motivation can be a real adventure.**

HOW KIDS COPE WITH STRESS

Don't place an emphasis on the specific behavior of a troubled kid as an indicator of what is wrong. Check out the situation in which the undesired behavior happens. And be sure to check out exactly how the kid perceives what is happening in the situation. A number of prominent therapists and researchers (Caplan, 1964; Ellis, 1973; and Lazarus, 1981) have pointed out that stress or crisis is not simply an event but a perception. Thus, while it may not be obvious to us that the situation of a kid demands the kind of behavior he exhibits, he may honestly see the situation entirely differently. When an inappropriate behavior doesn't relieve the stress a kid feels, but instead results in feelings of failure or feelings of increased rejection from peers, family, teachers or others, the kid begins attempting any behavior that might work. For as Mark Twain said,

Every man needs his own self approval.

Kids experiencing stress begin trial and error attempts to relate to others and feel good about themselves. It is during this trial and error phase that a kid may fall into a pattern of behavior that isolates him from his classmates and/or family and identifies him in the minds of his classmates and teachers as primarily a (1) verbal aggressor, (2) physical aggressor, (3) intimidator, (4) truant, (5) victim, (6) drug abuser, (7) delinquent, (8) general disrupter, (9) setter up (doing things that cause others to get into trouble), (10) depressed kid.

It has been my experience that almost none of the kids with whom I have worked set out to be one of the above problems. Rather, the kid became a problem by reacting to stress dysfunctionally. As Thomas Achenback (1982) has pointed out,

Abnormal behavior in its development doesn't differ essentially from normal behavior.

The only thing abnormal about most troubled kids with whom I've worked is that their use of problem solving skills is simply too restricted to address their problem. Despite his good intentions the kid is unable to find a workable solution to his problem. As a kid's limited use of problem solving skills fails, and he becomes more insecure, communication can become difficult. The kid begins to search less for solutions and has less hope of ever gaining help with his problems from others. The kid inwardly experiencing high stress settles on a limited range of short term coping behaviors. Or as Abraham

Maslow said,

> *When your only tool is a hammer,*
> *every problem looks like a nail.*

When a kid perceives himself to have failed or been rejected, he develops a fear of future failure. This can lead to anxiety and the wish to either withdraw from what or who he perceives as fearful and or the wish to aggress against the feared situation or person. The result is a negative social behavior which acts to produce a repetitive cycle of self-deprecation.

ENTERING THE CYCLE OF SELF DEPRECATION

The cycle basically starts with a stressful event.(See the stress flow chart on page 44.) Remember, stress generally is the degree of difference between what the kid expects to be the case and what he perceives to actually be the case. Step two in the cycle of the self-deprecation begins with the kid's attempt to break out of the stressful event. If he fails to cope, he then is likely to perceive himself as a failure or a rejected person. Step three in the cycle then is the result of dysfunctional thinking in which the kid equates failing at a task with being a failure. Step four is when the kid begins attempting by trial and error anything that might enable him to solve the problem and reduce his stress.

If step five is failure, then step six is that the kid increases his feelings of insecurity by reasoning that since is he failed in the past, he might very likely fail in future or be rejected. This kind of thinking may produce feelings in the kid of being inadequate, anxious, angry, attacked, hopeless or helpless. In step seven then, the kid may feel awful for a number of reasons. The eighth step is for the kid to blame himself and/or others for his pain. Unable to effectively resolve his problem, the kid is likely to take the ninth and final step of developing observable symptoms such as withdrawing socially, restricting his options, lowering his self esteem, over-reacting, acting out or becoming a perfectionist. Developing any of the step nine behavior styles usually leads to increased stress and reinforcement of the cycle.

Stress may be situation specific. A kid may be able to cope with stress at home for example and not be able to cope with stress at school. At home for example if something is stressing him out, he may simply get up and leave the room. At school if the kid attempts to use the coping mechanism of leaving the room and going for a walk he may find himself in an even more stressful situation because of having violated a school rule.

In this way, failures in learning lead to self deprecation, restriction of options in adapting and become future stressors. Failure in learning impedes future learning.

SELF DEPRECIATION CYCLE

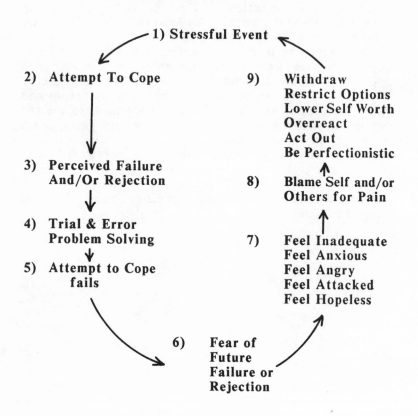

1) Stressful Event

2) Attempt To Cope

3) Perceived Failure
And/Or Rejection

4) Trial & Error
Problem Solving

5) Attempt to Cope
fails

6) Fear of
Future
Failure or
Rejection

7) Feel Inadequate
Feel Anxious
Feel Angry
Feel Attacked
Feel Hopeless

8) Blame Self and/or
Others for Pain

9) Withdraw
Restrict Options
Lower Self Worth
Overreact
Act Out
Be Perfectionistic

SUICIDE

Michelle: A Severe Case of Self-deprecation:River
Analogy

Michelle points up beautifully the crisis of self deprecation. She was a low ability middle school student who had been hospitalized for attempted suicide. Most people around her, including her parents, didn't appreciate the fact that she was cognitively limited. She had developed coping mechanisms for the daily demands of living. She made a point of closely modeling the clothes, speech and attitudes of those students she respected. Inside, she felt herself a failure. She couldn't fake academic achievement or social grace in new situations. Also, she couldn't talk to her folks about her problems because she didn't want to let them down. One day she just gave up hope and overdosed on her mother's medication.

The first step was to let Michelle disclose her feelings of inadequacy and failure. She spoke of how she'd studied long hours in order to pass tests that other kids could do in a snap. Her parents, she said, would comment that for all the hours she put in studying, she didn't get many high grades. At school, she felt on the outside of the group with whom she wanted to identify. Academically, teachers kept telling her that, if she just tried a little harder, she'd improve. Michelle disclosed that she was terrified of what awaited her socially and academically in high school. She felt she'd tried everything to cope and had been rejected. She blamed herself and overreacted.

I agreed with Michelle that her attempts at coping had not solved her problems; and in some cases, had even made things worse. But, I pointed out that only her methods had failed, not her. I also agreed that to go on trying to fake being smarter than she was, wouldn't work. She was absolutely right, I told her, in anticipating that high school would bring new social and intellectual challenges.

As we talked, I thought of an analogy by Loren Eisley in which he compared the evolution of man to a river. He said that the river twists, turns, moves slowly and then sometimes suddenly leaps violently ahead. He went on to say that the evolution of man is best described by the term, crisis.

I told Michelle that her life would be like a beautiful and powerful river with stretches when things seemed to flow beautifully and calmly, but that she would also come upon stretches of white water rapids. I told her that the wisest people were those who knew their weaknesses so that they could be ready for the rapids.

We talked about the signs that would tell her to seek help because rapids were approaching. She identified thoughts and feelings associated with anxiety and rejection. Then I told her that, **I would not think of attempting to take a boat down a river that might have rapids without a guide.**

As kids will do, Michelle asked who my guides were. I told her every couple of weeks, I had dinner with a very wise man who had lived much longer than I had. I told her that he was my model for the white water rapids that await me. Later, I involved the whole family as a support for Michelle. Getting the crisis out on the table rather than Michelle feeling she had to somehow cope with it all alone was in itself a tremendous stress reducer. Having an analogy to use in thinking about approaching crises reduced Michelle's tendency to panic and overreact.

WAYS A KID'S THINKING GETS DYSFUNCTIONAL

One of the keys to successful communication is understanding that the high stress experienced by the troubled kid is largely induced by the way he thinks. Simply put, the kid, by dysfunctional thinking processes, develops beliefs that distort the events of his life. For example, on the basis of another kid's bumping into him in the hall several times, the troubled kid might determine that the other student is against him. Or, if someone the troubled kid respects tells him the other kid is against him, the troubled kid might immediately take this on as a belief. The way a teacher by chance happens to move her eyes when talking to a troubled kid, might be an indication to the kid that the teacher doesn't like him. If an adult in the community has befriended the troubled kid and on some occasion speaks angrily to the kid, the kid might blow the whole episode up out of proportion and decide the man is no longer his friend.

The fact that dysfunctional thinking and the resultant faulty belief system should continue to be used by a kid when it obviously brings him much misery should not startle us. No matter how sharp our thinking, we all are capable of developing a nutty belief that can significantly interfere with our peace of mind.

For example, when a man is stuck in a traffic jam on a hot humid afternoon and needs desperately to get to a store before it closes, he can go from wondering what's holding traffic up to believing that without a doubt some dumb reason exists for the traffic jam. In such a situation, a man can become mean and irritable. However, if you inform such a person that you have come from up ahead and the traffic is being held up to help an injured child in the street, the man will probably cease to be angry and will probably apologize for having acted angry. In fact, some people who commute often even pre-empt stress by carrying a good book. They can look upon the traffic jam as an opportunity to read rather than a disaster.

Much research has been done on this relationship of language and thought to dysfunctional coping (Dollard and Miller, 1950; Lazarus, 1966; Beck, 1976; Meichenbaum, 1982). Several dysfunctional thinking styles that should be recognized are:

1) **Appeal to Authority**: Kids make faulty decisions by accepting on face value the statement of someone they respect.

2) **Over generalization**: Kids make a decision that doesn't work in other situations based solely on what they observed in one unique situation.

3) **Fantasizing** Unreal Expectations: Kids imagine what a situation is to be like based on what they would like or on what they fear, and then allow their fantasy to influence what happens.

4) **Arbitrary Inference**: Kids draw a faulty conclusion in the absence of sufficient evidence.

5) **Selective Editing**: Kids edit out or otherwise disregard an important factor in the situation.

6) **Blowing Out of Proportion**: Kids magnify or otherwise exaggerate the situation out of all proportion to its real meaning.

7) **Dichotomous Reasoning**: Kids think in black and white, either-or-terms. Either someone is for or against him.

8) **Unbounded Reality**: Anything not only is possible but has or will happen because kids wish it to. No additional factor except the kid's own internal fantasy is necessary for this type of thinking.

The types of dysfunctional thinking, or at least the specific one the individual kid practices, should be pointed out to the kid. The above eight ways of talking about faulty thinking can then serve as points of reference in discussions about what went wrong and why the kid is stressed out. In the absence of using these concrete landmarks, discussions with kids, particularly in times of crisis, may turn into pure ventilation or argument. An even worse situation is one in which the helper decides to think of the kid's faulty thinking as the kid's unique or creative way of approaching the world. This stamps a mark of approval on thinking that is getting the kid in trouble.

EMOTIONAL DISTURBANCE

Roger: An Extreme Case of Dysfunctional Thinking - Revolution Analogy

One of the most extreme forms of dysfunctional thinking that I have seen is that of a very bright kid named Roger. Roger's first psychological testing at age four had labeled him a time bomb just waiting to explode. Nevertheless, he had coasted along until the advent of puberty in middle school, shortly after which, he was kicked out of school and sent to a psychiatric facility. At the point I began counseling him, he had been released from the hospital into the hands of his single parent mother.

One of the first things I learned from Roger was the names and talents of all his favorite people. These included all of the people who indulged him in his distorted thinking. For example, he spoke warmly of several psychotherapists who had appeared to at least entertain the idea that Roger might be telepathic or even able to do telekinesis. In our first session, it was clear that Roger wanted to see if I would buy into what he called "thought control". My intention with Roger, as with practically all kids evidencing extreme thought dysfunction, is to do empathic responding in the first session just to see how far the kid will go. I suspended my disbelief as I frequently do at a play and allowed myself to enjoy the kid's performance. I did not however get sucked into his nutty beliefs.

Roger told me of ghosts that appeared to him and of talking to a friend by telepathy. The ultimate extreme was when Roger informed me that he had taken pictures of a cat which reappeared two weeks after dying. When I asked if I could see the picture, Roger informed me that it was strange how his best pictures got lost!

USING A ROCK MUSIC ANALOGY

In the first session, **we spent some time talking about the kinds of music Roger liked, which eventually led to a discussion about the Beatles' song** *Revolution.* **Roger took the meaning of the song literally. He felt that the Beatles wanted to have a very aggressive, if not violent, revolution. I disagreed, and we had a discussion about paradoxical talk and mixed messages in song. It became an anchor for my talks with Roger. When he'd start talking in mixed messages or word salad, I'd ask if the revolution was on again.** Often he'd become very rational and demonstrate that he could express himself clearly, or he'd ask what was mixed up about what he was saying.

In later sessions, I informed Roger in very clear terms that talking of weird things including suicide, a favorite topic, while fun to do wouldn't be allowed in our sessions. I told him that he would gain friends, meet girls, and get along better educationally and career wise, by dropping his nutty talk. I told him that, in fact, most people would consider anyone crazy and not want to have anything to do with him if he talked too nutty. I told him I was, in fact, interested in parapsychology and that some day when I heard that he was really clear headed and a very sharp thinker, then we could again have a discussion about these far out topics.

STOPPING THOUGHTS

Every time that Roger began talking about weird things, I'd yell, "Stop the revolution!" or just "Stop!" This is called **thought stopping**. It worked beautifully with

Roger. After about six months, he'd virtually stopped trying out his weird ideas on me and others. He could see that, in fact, he made more friends by not being quite so weird. Then, I began to be able to confront his basic dysfunctional thought style which was **dichotomous reasoning.** As Roger tried to describe the experiences of his life in blacks and whites where he believed people were either for or against him, I challenged Roger to look at the grays and to realize there were often many factors leading to any given action by another person he encountered. We worked together with me unrelentingly challenging Roger's beliefs. Roger did eventually learn to stop both his weird talk as well as dichotomous reasoning. He graduated from high school and has worked at odd jobs off and on.

I don't want to imply by this illustration that there is some quick and easy way to remove the troubles of a "psychotic kid." In fact, it may be that "true" psychosis results at least in part from a biochemical imbalance or disease of the brain. I do mean for this to illustrate that most of Roger's difficulties resulted from his belief that his distorted way of thinking was valid, valuable or even superior to other ways of thinking. I do mean for this to illustrate that Roger thought he was gaining important recognition for his nutty ideas. Thus it was important for me to say the right thing to Roger because it gave him a reason to want to clear up his thinking. The point is not that using analogies with Roger cured him of a serious psychiatric problem but that it motivated him to begin trying to communicate and act more functionally. It got him to listen maybe for the first time in his life. As a result, he functioned better with others. As others spent more time with Roger, he enjoyed life more. Enjoying life more led to a less stressful life.

It's hard for me to imagine someone saying the right things to someone as disturbed as Roger unless that person was able to get into Roger's rhythms. It was important in working with Roger successfully to be able to use his metaphors, *revolution* for example, to frame analogies for him to then use in clarifying his thinking. As Milton

Erickson said,

> *It isn't the theory of psychotherapy.*
> *It's how you reach the personality by*
> *saying the right thing at the right time.*

FANTASIES

It is difficult to know what are the most important factors to consider in helping kids. It is clear whatever they are they occur in his head,in the thoughts, feelings and fantasies that he rarely if ever shares with anyone. Troubled kids tend to be isolated from close relationships; and so their most important dialogue about life events are private and unavailable. As Mark Twain said speaking of people in general:

> *What a wee little part of a person's life*
> *are his acts and his words! His real life*
> *is led in his head. And is known to none*
> *but himself.*

How much more true for a kid who perceives the exterior world as punishing or stressful at the very least. How strongly will the troubled kid protect against intrusions into what he considers most dear? The answer is, very strongly! Some kids commit suicide rather than reveal what's important in their interior world.

Even the people the kid comes to like and respect may be forbidden easy entry into his interior world. And on occasion if the kid perceives someone entering his world, he may react swiftly, aggressively and irrationally. The story of Bubbles is a case in point.

52

RAGE REACTIONS

Bubbles: A Case of Abuse and Rejection--Island Animal Analogy

Bubbles was a regular student who was great to be around most of the time. About every one or two weeks, she would "blow up" and begin refusing to do what anyone told her, and would verbally or physically abuse anyone who decided to confront her. One minute Bubbles seemed fine, and the next she was a raging animal, which is what led a school counselor to call me for advice. He thought maybe she was having some kind of seizure, and that a neurological evaluation and medication was in order.

On the day he called me, Bubbles had refused to stop in the hall when a teacher called to her; and then when a vice principal who just happened to pass by attempted to stop her, she hit him. The teacher said she was just trying to tell Bubbles what a good job she had done on a class project. Bubbles didn't calm down for about an hour, and she wouldn't talk about why she acted as she had. Bubbles behavior was frighteningly erie to the staff.

In fact, the teacher had intruded on Bubbles' interior world by complete accident when she called to Bubbles and told her to stop. From inside the confused interior world Bubbles inhabited, she heard the teacher's voice as a command of an aggressor. Bubbles, as I was to find out, felt rejected by her mother when she was a young child. She felt both anger toward her mother as well as guilt for possibly causing the rejection. As Bubbles walked down the hall of the school that afternoon, the blurred memories and expectations that she dragged with her from an earlier age mingled with the events of more recent days to produce an immature and nebulous sense of identity. She wavered between guilt, self-righteousness, openness to help, and withdrawal, in fear of losing control of her shaky grasp on reality. Her tough exterior, however, hid any sign of her fragility. Expectations conditioned by past events led to behavior which provoked rejection rather than the affection she sought.

She experienced others' reactions to her as confusing and as confirmation of the rejection she had learned to expect. In the face of too much perceived conflict and stress, she regressed to earlier levels of social adaptation.

Like a two year old, she lashed out verbally or physically and then withdrew. Her memories of abuse and rejection were perplexing. Her current perceptions were at times distorted by the dark wavering lens of the past. Periodically, during developmental crises or times of perceived stress, her image of a rational orderly state of things dissolved into confused consciousness.

With Bubbles, **I used the analogy of the danger of getting cramps while swimming alone.**

> *I told her a story of someone I knew who died from a cramp while swimming alone. We talked about how important it was to keep friends around at almost any cost.*

Eventually, I got her to practice closing her eyes, entering a private world, and finding an imaginary friend who could support her in facing the real world. The point is that strong people feel that there is something special inside them that nothing can extinguish.

> *I told her it was important to always keep a special feeling that deep inside there was a friend like a warm sun that would be with her no matter what she should face.*

The reason an imaginary support system can work is because it can spark positive thinking. Bubbles was wonderful to be around when she was positive.

Bernie Siegel(1986) a surgeon and professor at Yale University School of Medicine in his powerful best seller titled *Love, Medicine and Miracles* goes so far as to say that positive images are a way of enlisting the unconscious in the process of changing one's behavior significantly enough to not only alter one's mood and relationships with others but to help prevent and cure life threatening illnesses.

Even with the untroubled kid, feelings are sometimes easily hurt by a word poorly chosen. What begins one minute as a mature discussion, can in another minute turn into a raging war. For this reason, anyone would do well to follow some guidelines for having discussions with kids so as not to violate what's important to the kid's internal world. I have found the following guidelines useful as a rule of thumb.

COMMUNICATING PRODUCTIVELY WITH KIDS

1) **Do Not Engage In Power Struggles**.
Let the kid win whenever you possibly can. Let him feel he won. In fact, say to him, "There you go again. You won another one."

2) **Never Attack The Kid or His Friends Personally**. Make sure you can concretely defend your position. For example, you can say, "None of your friends may smoke while in my house," but you can't say I don't like people who smoke in my house.

3) **Choose Your Language Carefully**.
For example, you can say, "The bedroom must be clean to my satisfaction on Saturday morning before you can go out." You can't say, "Look, it's only Monday and already the room looks like a dump."

4) **Establish A Logical Formula For How You Can Be Defeated**. The object here is for the kid to learn to prepare arguments and to attempt to carry them through rationally in order to win verbal battles. You should have standard beliefs you argue over again and again. As he becomes more logical in his thinking he'll become less confused. Say, "I understand or I don't understand your thinking." Don't say, "I simply feel differently and that's all there is to it."

5) **Use Humor**. When things get heavy, use humor. However, a word of caution: Do not use humor unless you are good at it. Attempted humor can easily be seen as sarcasm by misplaced tone, emphasis or gestures. Sarcasm will further enrage an angry kid.

6) **Question Everything**. Don't accept statements of authority or statements such as, "the research says." Say,"I know this sounds dumb but my dad taught me to always demand the facts and in his memory I always do that. Can you tell me your source and the facts?"

7) **Don't Accept Correlations As Cause**. It is almost impossible really to prove anything. However, do not accept statements such as, "Everybody else's parents allow it, so it must be okay." It can also be that either all the parents don't allow it; or, if they do, they don't understand what's going on, or they do it because of intimidation.

8) **Ignorance Is One Of The Greatest Tools In Counseling**. To restructure the argument or take a different look say, "What is your argument anyhow?"

9) **Help Clarify The kid's Thoughts**. To help the kid clarify his thoughts, you could say, "I wonder if you could say that over in a different way so that I can understand."

10) **Question The Value Of Dysfunctional Behavior.** Say to a blamer, "What are the benefits of blaming it on him?" Say to someone who says that he doesn't care what anyone thinks, "Do you think you'll succeed without needing anyone?"

11) **Step Outside The Argument To Gain Perspective**. Encourage the person to drop the intensity of the argument by looking at it as though he and you were gods on Olympus. For example, say, "Let's imagine you and I were scientists looking at an experiment."

12) **Always Respect The Kid**.   Don't say, "This is ridiculous."   Under proper circumstances, you might confront by saying, "I'm going to take a chance and tell you what I really think about this."

13) **Use Paradox And Catastrophe To Promote Positive Ends**.   Say, "It sounds like you're telling me you're impossible to change." The youth will have to try to prove that he is able to change in order to continue attempting to win the argument.

14) **Show What Your Interests Are**.   Be energetic and excited about things that matter to you. Kids need to know that you think there are events in your life that are the most important things anyone could be doing.

15) **Take An Action To Show You Are Capable Of Change**. If a kid mentions a book he likes, read it. If he mentions a song he likes, listen to it. If he mentions an activity, when appropriate, try it. Let him know you did those things by discussing your experiences with him.

16) **Do Not Talk About Making A kid Happy or Successful**. You can't do either and most kids know it.

17) **Tell Brief Tales Of Life That Are Interesting To The Kid**. Use these as metaphors for the kid to use in interpreting the events of his life and constructing his own myth for the future.

18) **Choose Your Battles**.   If you battle on concerns of lesser importance, you will be seen a nagger, perhaps the worst enemy of adolescence.

19) **Put It On Paper**.   Write down your agreements so that you have a reference and don't end up arguing about a previous . discussion.

20) **Exit Loud And Angry Arguments**.   Don't engage in threats and open hostility. Simply excuse yourself for a

good reason such as needing to make a call or go to the bathroom. The passage of time itself can reduce the tension level.

21) **Be Assertive**. Don't accept responsibility for not playing a role assigned you by the kid. Do state concretely what is acceptable and what is not acceptable.

22) **Don't Take It For Granted That You Are Understood.**

23) **Don't Lecture**. State your idea or your opinion and perhaps the law of your home but not a universal law.

24) **Keep An Open Mind**.

CONCLUSION

When merely being himself gets a kid in constant trouble with others, he has a problem. It may be that his heart is in the right place, and he is not setting out to be a problem. In fact it may be that the problem is one of his entire ecosystem, consisting of family, community and school. Nicole, the young girl who was cutting herself on the arms as a way of dealing with stress is an excellent example. It was a tragic situation in which she and her family both felt they were doing everything possible to make things work. All the while, Nicole was doing herself in. As it turned out, the family needed an analogy in order to fully understand and focus on how they were helping set in motion Nicole's self-injurious acts. Family dynamics can be as difficult and frustrating to sort out as a tangle of strings. Analogy can cut through the tangle.

4

CONFRONTING KIDS

*"If you kick a stone, you can predict the trajectory
of the stone. This is not true of kicking dogs."*

Richard Lazarus

WHEN CONFRONTING A KID, I HAVE FOUND IT
USEFUL TO THINK OF THE KID AS LOST IN A GAME
OF HIDE AND SEEK IN WHICH THE KID FEELS HE
HAS BEEN DOWN MANY CONVOLUTED PASSAGES
IN LIFE AND HAS LOST THE THREAD THAT WOULD
LEAD HIM BACK TO THE MAIN ROAD.

An assumption I make is that while the passages of
the kid's life may seem disjointed and different, they in
fact all lead back to some central urging of the kid's true
self. Metaphors, images and analogies, as Carl Jung and
Joseph Campbell among others point out, can help resolve
the apparently conflicting parts of ourselves.

**I use analogy to confront the kid because it allows the
kid to untangle the conflicts of his life in the here and
now.** The intent in confronting a kid with analogy is to
help a kid alter the way, even very slightly, in which he
has been perceiving the designs in the material of his life.

It is clear that, in order to significantly change a kid's
mind, we must change his perception. As Emerson said,

"We perceive what we are prepared to perceive."

Kids constantly carry on conversations with themselves to attempt to clarify what is happening to them. As Anne Frank wrote in her diary,

I think what is happening to me is so wonderful, and not only what can be seen on my body, but all that is taking place inside me. I never discuss myself or any of these things with anybody; that is why I have to talk to myself about them.

It is important to recognize the importance of landmarks in the game of hide-and-seek kids play with themselves. The stories become landmarks for the kid to use to keep from getting lost in his old dysfunctional thoughts. The **analogies act as landmarks** to remind the kid that it is not the passages of his life that are confusing, but rather his clumsy thinking about what is happening to him.

STARING IN WONDER

Analogies also act as models for the kid to imitate when no parent or other helper is around to assist him. The wise use of analogies enables the kid to model positive expectations without a parent. The material of stories and analogies is mostly the ordinary events of everyday life. It is a central tenet of using analogies that the kid and parent delight and marvel at the ordinary events of life: controlling a baseball pitch; picking up a glass of water; lighting a fire; emptying a purse; dunking a tea bag; getting unstuck in a briar patch. The way of analogies allows the kid to appreciate the wisdom that nature has clothed in the ordinary mundane events of life. This process of staring at the ordinary and finding new meaning for oneself is exhilarating in and of itself.

For many kids, simply beginning the process of searching for interesting new colors and threads in the tapestry of life's ordinary everyday events is a major transformation. It can take a kid out of a self-conscious

approach overly concerned with his own appearances to a sense of wonder at the possibilities that lie outside himself.

Wise use of analogies then holds the power to make a kid realize that he is staring at something very different from what he expected. Once a kid has this experience, it is then hard for him to continue to act and think in dysfunctional ways. It is difficult to remain stuck in the same old dysfunctional ways that upset others, once one has begun to approach life as a room full of wonderful clothes and costumes in which it is both safe and fun to lose oneself.

The analogies and images presented here don't pretend to be complex, finely designed and finished products.They are often a patch work of disjointed events; the clothes of a person's life. The analogies and images are pieced together as collaboration with the kid dictates.

The brief analogies,quips, and tales serve as gestures or directions for getting on with the plot. They are clearly not the whole story. In fact when working with very troubled adolescents, I prefer to use analogies in conjunction with a highly individualized therapeutic school program, individualized cognitive-behavioral counseling and a strategic family therapy program. The wise use of analogies then is a way for learning how to knit the events of our life together, accept the patchwork design for its own self, then be able to throw it on and go have a look at the world. In short, a kid needs to feel good about how others see him and about how he sees himself.

A good analogy to keep in mind when working with kids is that of sailing. If your destination is dead into the wind, you have to tack toward it. For those of you who don't sail, this means that you have to sail first from one side, then to the other, zigzagging, bit by bit, toward your destination so that you never head straight into the wind. If you were to head into the wind, you would put your boat "in-irons." The sail would flap about uselessly and the boat would stop dead.

> *It's frustrating business not being*
> *able to head directly toward your goal*
> *when you're eager to get there but*
> *sometimes a sideways approach is the*
> *only way.*

Trying to make a head on assault on a kid's beliefs can leave you feeling that you're locked in-irons. As in the sailing anecdote, the more you attempt to get directly to the problem, the more resistance the kid seems to present. This sailing technique of going sideways, or tacking, is the only way, however slow, to make any gain toward your goal with extremely oppositional adolescents. It is a true key to communicating with kids.

HEAD ON ASSAULT ON A KID'S BELIEFS

The trouble with just going straight forward and providing information that discredits a kid's belief is that people will continue believing even when the facts don't fit their beliefs. I'm not just talking about kids. James W. Lichtenberg (1984) cites a number of studies in a fascinating paper which suggests that people may even strengthen their beliefs and become more polarized when presented with strong empirical evidence which discredits their beliefs. One interesting example cited was that from a study conducted by Ross, Lepper and Hubbard (1976),in which academic types were given strong positive feed back about their performance on a task. Later after being shown data that clearly debunked the earlier good feedback, the participants continued to rate their skills on the basis of the bogus positive feedback.

I'm not here suggesting that anyone should give up on being explicit and straightforward with a kid when attempting to challenge his beliefs. In fact, I feel the Rational Emotive Strategy of Albert Ellis (1962), which makes much use of confronting irrational beliefs head on, when used properly is a powerful strategy for confronting kids. I'm just suggesting that it helps to have a way to make the discrediting of a kid's irrational beliefs palatable to the kid. And, given that normal academic types are capable of continuing to believe even when the facts don't fit, the subtle use of analogy offers what on occasion may be the only hope of getting the message through.

Anyone who interacts with kids will on occasion feel that a kid is maliciously refusing to let any messages through. And, in the case of some sociopathic kids, that is probably the case. I'm convinced that with most of the kids we see, no matter what their outward actions and words, they cling tightly to inappropriate behavior as a final safety line in a world of insecurity and frustration. The troubled kid separates himself from appropriate social interaction foolishly thinking that his only hope of avoiding frustration is either to withdraw from or dominate people. In either case, he acts inappropriately out of the mistaken notion that by doing so he can maintain some control over his life. In doing so, he pits himself against the mainstream of society. He has the mistaken notion that he can't function in the world without dominating it.

The point is that kids sometimes attempt to relieve stress by becoming a closed system focused on dominating potential stressors and, by doing so, in fact insure that they will be frustrated. The well selected analogy confronts by not presenting itself as potentially stressful. It confronts in the form of stories, images and metaphors about nonthreatening things of interest to kid. **In listening to analogy, the kid is not wondering, "Am I going to be pressured to answer something that I'm not sure how to answer?"** The kid can join in thinking about an interesting image or story which is not overtly related to any problem he might have. For example, take the case of Tommy.

DEPRESSION

TOMMY: An Out-of-Control Depression - Hero Analogy

This young man with whom I worked felt that the world treated him extremely unfairly. According to Tommy, everyone was against him, and he had good reason for being angry and aggressive. As an infant, he had open heart surgery which restricted his physical activity through his younger years. It worried him deeply that his parents constantly threatened each other with divorce. And he hadn't learned well in school. The fact that he had to live in such unfair circumstances perhaps made him oversensitive to the slightest kind of unfairness on the part of his teachers, particularly if the teacher unknowingly used certain words that Tommy had attached to the arguments and problems in his family. Often, well meaning teachers, while attempting to convey positive feelings toward him, had upset him terribly.

A person seeking to help Tommy might decide to confront Tommy on the issue of unfairness. However, if the helper attempted to do so by sitting down and asking Tommy why he always felt on the defensive for example, then the person would find himself with a stubborn kid who would refuse to talk about the issue of unfairness. If the helper chose to press the issue, then the helper would likely find Tommy going out of control, yelling, threatening, throwing things and walking out.

A helper using analogy would have listened carefully to what Tommy liked and how he communicated. He would have found that Tommy loved physical activity and loved to talk about sports and adventure. The helper would have devised a story or analogy around the issue of unfairness. The story could just pop out in one of his talks with Tommy about sports or outdoor adventures. The analogy would have to be removed from any direct relationship to the issue of unfairness and yet contain all the necessary components to enable Tommy to use the analogy to confront the issue of unfairness on his own or with a little help from someone. One could talk with Tommy about quicksand.

*Imagine if you and a friend were hiking in
the woods and suddenly found your feet sinking
in a moist sandy earth that sucked you down
deeper and deeper as you tried to escape.
What would you do to save your life?*

Tommy would have to get beyond the fact that it was unfair for him to be caught up in the treacherous force. He would have to acknowledge that his traditional way of coping with his feet being stuck wasn't going to work. He'd have to open his mind to a different way of reacting to the crisis. When he finally figured out that force was counterproductive, the object would be for Tommy to draw an analogy to his own problem.

The helper might decide on another analogy in which someone is being overpowered and the attempt to rescue himself by fighting the overpowering force would merely insure defeat. Because Tommy liked baseball, a good story would be that of Jackie Robinson.

*He was the first black baseball player to
break into the major leagues. He couldn't
fight the prejudice directly; but, by
controlling himself and becoming a great
baseball player, he indirectly helped
weaken racism. He appealed to something the
racists could understand -- baseball.*

This story could just pop up in a conversation with Tommy about outdoor adventures or the helper could guide Tommy's discussion to issues of courage. Tommy could either just be left with the story; or, if appropriate, the story could be discussed with Tommy.

The point here is not that having heard this story Tommy would immediately cease to be upset and cease to act out around issues of unfairness. In fact, I ended up having similar discussions many times and doing many crisis interventions with Tommy and his family before Tommy started to change. I made reference to the Jackie

Robinson story again and again. The point is that the story gave Tommy a place to begin to get unstuck. It's like the tab on a fresh roll of tape. Without it it's hard to get started. The analogy was something that he and I could come back to in crisis interventions when he was fighting a world he considered to be unfair. Tommy's family was able to use the story to size up their situation as a family. They were caught up in something stronger than themselves and needed to learn how to cope. Kids like Tommy are open to stories and remember stories. In fact, Tommy later told me that he'd used the story with several of his friends.

Analogies can plant seeds of change by enabling a kid to sense that something is just a bit amiss with the way he's approaching life. Charmaine is a girl whose case points to the power of analogy in planting seeds of change.

ANTI-SOCIAL PERSONALITY

CHARMAINE: Case of a Gang Leader--Baseball Analogy
Charmaine was a very pretty 16 year old girl who dressed and acted tough and unfeminine. In fact her mother thought Charmaine had gender identity problems. When I first met her, Charmaine described herself as a trainer of other girls in school. She would set up girls to fight each other. Her tactic was to start a rumor which would set in motion the particular fight she wished to see. A group of girls reinforced her behavior by respecting her as a leader. Being able to manipulate others gave her a sense of control when she was very insecure.

Charmaine was a bright girl who felt insecure about her looks and ability to be accepted, so she set herself in conflict with others, not ever giving others a chance to show acceptance toward her. In fact, when anyone, peer or teacher, other than her gang of girls attempted to befriend her, she reacted aggressively.

A way to think about Charmaine's problem is to

imagine a baseball pitcher who demands that he have perfect control. The baseball pitcher's situation is hopeless because if he even attempts to throw the ball at all he'll lose some control. Once the ball is thrown it is "out of his hands." It's a frustrating situation to put oneself into, and it's the way Charmaine had attempted to solve her problems.

She confined her socialization to a very narrow circle of peers over whom she exerted total domination and control. Eventually over a period of years a female counselor built a relationship with Charmaine that helped Charmaine change. One of the self instructional techniques that the counselor used with Charmaine was to have her say to herself,

*"I can't demand that I have complete control
because that would mean I would be like a baseball
pitcher who could never play a game for fear of
failing if he throws one bad pitch ."*

The strategy was to hook Charmaine into a relationship outside of her narrow circle. Use of analogy helped her to see that her striving for perfect security was robbing her of a real sense of security.

The remainder of this chapter is an anthology of analogies that address a number of typical adolescent complaints, arguments and beliefs.

*It is important to know that these analogies
are differentiated by presenting statement only
as an example. In nearly all cases, the analogy
or image will have to be tailored to the particular
interaction with the kid at hand if it is to have
any lasting power. .*

ANALOGIES FOR CONFRONTATIONS WITH KIDS

The Old Father

Kid Says: "I can't tell him because it would hurt his feelings."

There is a story about a man who had been a hero in an earlier French war and was living in a small French village during the Second World War. His children lived in the village with him. He never left the house where he lived because he had become too old and too ill to do so. He spent most of his time buoyed by his memories of the past, so his children wished to protect him from knowing the horrible truth that the Germans were slowly overrunning France. Whenever he would ask how the war was going, they would tell him it was going just great. He was sort of isolated and had no access to other information. He was happy to learn from his children that things were going well and that the government of his country, in which he believed so deeply, was doing well. Then one day, as he was waking, he looked out across the way and actually saw the Germans entering the city. He realized that his children had been lying to him, and with that he had a heart attack and died.

DISCUSSION: Can we really protect anyone ultimately? Is it not true that sometimes the side effects from protection can be worse than the evil from which we seek to protect the person.

* * * * * *

A Pile of Manure

Kid Says: "I know what I want to do."

One of America's greatest writers, Nathanial Hawthorne, once went off to live with a group of other people on a farm commune in New England. This was a long time ago. But the reality of farm work didn't fit his romantic picture of it. He went there because it looked like a beautiful way to live, a way that he could get his writing done, live around some wonderful people and not be plagued by all the other problems of living. He soon left, saying to a friend, "I didn't come here to live under a pile of manure."

*   *   *   *   *   *

Tough Times Help

Kid Says: "My life hasn't been easy."

I once read about a lady who literally had a huge crane fall on her in New York City, crushing her legs and pinning her down to dangle precariously from a high bridge. The doctors all said that the reason she survived was because she had a lot of other tough times in her life. She had fallen from a ski lift. She'd been in a number of awful situations, and she responded with a tremendously clear, happy, functional state of mind and a strong will to continue. She attributed her success to the fact that she had grown stronger from her earlier problems.

DISCUSSION: Some tough times can help one become strong. Then there's also the story of the broken leg and how, when it mends, it's stronger than before it was broken. This is a discussion around the idea of tough times so as to reframe them as something positive.

*   *   *   *   *   *

A Bundle

Kid Says: "I've got too many problems."

The best way to break a bundle of sticks is one by one.

DISCUSSION: Should center around assessment of the various difficulties and prioritizing the problems so that they can be taken on one by one.

*   *   *   *   *   *

The Road Of Life

Kid Says: "I'm having a real tough time with my life."

The road of life has been compared to a highway with ruts that cannot be seen but only felt.

DISCUSSION: The really tough problems in life are not those that can be easily seen and preempted and prepared for. They're the ones that come along and you slam into them. You look back, and you realize you ran over a great big hole in the road.

* * * * * *

Good Models

Kid Says: "I don't know if I can bear it."

You know however bad you might find things, it's important to have models, people who've been through some pretty terrible things and handled the situation wisely. An example would be Anne Frank, and I would suggest you read her book. It's the story of a little girl who had to hide out in an attic during the time of the Nazis. She lived in Holland in Amsterdam. The Nazis had taken over her country and the city of Amsterdam, and she and her family hid out together. In her book, she never once ceased to be optimistic despite the fact that her very life was at stake almost every minute, and eventually she was in fact found out by the Nazis. They took her and put her in a concentration camp where she died. It is important to know that she never ceased to believe that life was good. It is this kind of story that's important to read when you come to the point of saying I don't know if I can bear it.

DISCUSSION: Simply discuss how bad are things after all? What's the worst that could happen?

* * * * * *

The Bull Of Athens

Kid Says: "I don't think I'll ever be able to do what I am trying to do. It's just too big a task for me."

A folk tale of Athens tells of a person who was very strong and could lift a 2,000 pound bull. When asked how he could possibly come to do that, he said that when he was a young boy and the bull was a baby, every day he began to lift the bull. As the bull grew older, he was always able to pick it up the next day because it only weighed a little bit more. He said finally it got to be 2,000 pounds and he was still picking it up.

DISCUSSION: Of course I don't believe the story is true, but it points out the need to learn in very small steps. Kids often want to do everything at once. They should break down the task and space it into small incremental steps. Success breeds success.

* * * * * *

Good Pain

Kid Says: "I don't know why I harm myself now and then. I cut myself, do things to myself."

There is no pain that you can ever use to make yourself feel good.

DISCUSSION: Why does a kid harm himself? What does he think he is going to get out of it? To what is the pain directed? Is it directed at your family? Is it directed at a failure of yours? Has it developed because of a condition such as unfairness?

* * * * * *

Independent Children

Kid Says: "I don't need anyone."

Have you ever noticed how independent children can be until they get sick. Along with its joys, life is a series of threats I wouldn't want to face alone.

DISCUSSION: What does the person really mean since

we know everyone needs someone? What is it that the person is really trying to say with, "I don't need anyone." And does the person really want to put himself in some kind of vulnerable situation and get hurt? And why would he want to do that?

* * * * * *

Traveling Alone
Kid Says: "It's no fun being alone."

Sometimes the path in life narrows so much that you are required to go on alone. But also it has been said that he travels fastest who travels alone.
DISCUSSION: Center discussion around issues of being alone and using being alone to get things accomplished. Talk about there being a reason for being alone.

* * * * * *

Performing
Kid Says: "My life is dull."

Maybe you have been thinking life as an auditorium rather than a stage. You've been waiting for someone else to perform.
DISCUSSION: You might talk about the kid's life and how he traps himself. Talk to him about becoming more imaginative as a matter of the way he lives. Talk to him about making things happen. Together you might come up with a little experiment he could perform to make himself freer. He might go do some window shopping in places where he wouldn't normally think of buying anything. He might begin to just wear one article of clothing differently. Just get him to change his life in little ways to break boundaries of different kinds so that he can begin to change his whole way of approaching life. Get him to take action.

* * * * * *

Program of Life

Kid Says: "If someone would just tell me what to do."
In the concert of life, there is no program.
DISCUSSION: Talk about how life keeps changing. There can't be any fixed ways of doing things because you have to be able to individualize and deal with the context of life that just keeps changing on everybody.

* * * * * *

Puppet

Kid Says: "I just go along with it even though I think it's dumb."
Do you want to be a puppet having someone pull your strings to make you dance?
DISCUSSION: Going along with things can be a very weak act of someone who is willing to be just a puppet on a string. Do you want to have no thoughts or choices of your own, but merely react?

* * * * * *

Mountain Trails

Kid Says: "I don't seem to be getting anywhere."
It may be impossible to go straight   up   the mountainside, but sometimes you can wind your way up. In fact, it is pretty tough to go straight from one place to another anywhere.
DISCUSSION: Center around where you are trying to get to and how you have been trying to get there. Have you been trying to go straight ahead? Maybe that's the problem.

* * * * * *

Kindling

Kid Says: "I never finish anything."

A match is great for getting things going, but without proper follow up with kindling and wood, it is almost useless in the long run.

DISCUSSION: Use the metaphor of the kindling of the wood to get at what the person needs to use as kindling and wood to finish up tasks that are started.

* * * * * *

Worse Than Before

Kid Says: "I have trouble finishing."

You know you can use soap to clean the plate, but if you don't rinse it, it's worse than before you started.

DISCUSSION: There's also the idea that if you start something and don't finish, you can leave whatever you started worse off than if you'd left it alone. Think about the time you began a task and then didn't have time to finish.

* * * * * *

Catching Monkeys

Kid Says: "I'm not giving an inch."

You know they say that one of the ways of catching monkeys in Africa is to drop fruit in a knothole of a tree. The monkey sticks his hand and then makes a fist around the fruit. He then can't pull out his fist until he gives up the fruit. Some monkeys get caught rather than give up the fruit. Sometimes you must drop the old to pursue the new. You might tell the story of having watched a little child on the beach becoming very frustrated picking up pebbles and shells. She was frustrated because, in order to pick one up, she had to drop one.

DISCUSSION: Centers around letting go in order to be free to change or to get something else that is more important in one's life.

Poetry and Biochemistry

Kid Says: "How do you change the way you see things?"

I once heard a man who'd won the Nobel Prize in biochemistry say that he was going to start reading poetry and try to change the way he thought about things so that the next time he looked in the microscope or he read a paper or sat and thought about what he was doing, he'd come up with some new ideas.

DISCUSSION: Explore how changing what you do can change the way you see the world.

* * * * * *

A Good Way To Think

Kid Says: "How do you problem solve?"

When you are hunting for Easter eggs, do you have to come at them from different directions?

DISCUSSION: Talk about the many ways to problem solve. Go ahead and list everything, the wildest, craziest possible things. Get into the habit of considering everything. Then go back and scratch out one by one the ones whose results don't appeal to you. It may be that what you are left with won't be very appealing either, but you'll know it's the best of the worst choices. This is, in fact the only way you can arrive at what action to take in situations for which there are no good solutions.

* * * * * *

Dieseling

Kid Says: "It's hard to control myself."

You know it is important for a car to run well, but it is considered a problem if it diesels, keeps on running after it is supposed to stop and rest.

DISCUSSION: Do athletes preparing for races run as long and hard as they can in practice? Did you know that field goal kickers in the National Football League limit the number of practice kicks so as not to burn out or tire out? Wonder if it has anything to do with what they tell themselves?

* * * * * *

Runaway
Kid says: "I'm gonna run away, unless things change around here."

You could escape earth's gravity by going to the moon, but when you return, the gravity would be waiting. I don't want you to run away; but, if you should succeed in doing so, know that when you decide to return, we'll be happy to have you back. However, our rules will still be enforced.

DISCUSSION: Is it really us you are running away from? What is it that you really need to get away from? Can we be of any help in freeing you from what's bugging you? Would you like to see a counselor with us to negotiate.

* * * * * *

Try Too Hard
Kid Says: "Everyone says I take it too seriously."

Have you ever seen a little kid kick so hard he lands upon his ass?

DISCUSSION: Ever try to remember something and the more you tried, the harder it seemed; but, then when you quit trying, you remembered it.

* * * * * *

Within You
Kid Says: "How can I live with what's happened?"

What lies behind you and what lies before are nothing compared with what lies within you.

DISCUSSION: Is it possible that you have potential that

you haven't discovered? Have you ever looked seriously and deeply within yourself for values to get you through? Did you know that a great man named Ranier Marie Rilke once said we should use our sorrows to grow rather than try to get rid of them.

* * * * * *

Old Potatoes

Kid Says: "Things used to be easier."

Once I visited a man who lived on a houseboat, and he told me the following story. He said that he was very fond of eating potatoes from his family garden when he was a boy in England. Lately, he longed for the taste of one of those potatoes. So, he went back home and tried one. He was surprised, he said, to find out that the potatoes tasted just like the ones he bought in Sausalito. Apparently, he had changed, not the potatoes. DISCUSSION: We change slowly not realizing it. Do you remember exactly when you stopped playing with your childhood toys?

* * * * * *

Turning Sideways

Kid Says: "No matter what I do, we fight."

When a wolf wants to preempt a fight, he turns sideways to his would-be opponent. By making himself more vulnerable he signals that he himself does not intend to attack and so defuses the other wolf's aggression. Maybe you need to turn sideways in your relationship somehow. DISCUSSION: Are you waiting for the other person to change or for some magical solution? Is it possible that you will have to take some unilateral action?

* * * * * *

Chasing The Future
Kid Says: "There's no future for me."

I once heard an old Hopi Indian in Arizona say that the future is always running away from a person and they must race after it if they are to expect to catch it.

DISCUSSION: It requires energy, commitment, hard work, and even a willingness to experience failure in order to succeed.

CONCLUSION

Communicating with kids can get frustrating because every time you think you have the issues pinned down, the wind seems to come out of nowhere and scatter all your work. Often it's tough to carry on a meaningful discussion with kids because they want to talk all around the issue rather than go straight at it. Kids are operating on a different time scale. They usually don't feel the urgency to get to the bottom of things in the way that those helping them might. In addition, kids often have unusual agendas. What might seem least important to a parent or counselor may be of primary importance to a kid.

When you decide to confront a kid, know that no matter how good your evidence, you may end up losing. In fact, if your evidence is unassailable and the kid knows it, he may become even more polarized in his view. Kids, like others, are capable of strengthening their views when the facts don't fit rather than getting rid of their faulty ideas. Since analogies allow for the kid to assimilate the conflicting evidence in his own manner in his own time, it can be the best way to confront. An analogy must be tailored to the kid's problem. The analogy, when done well however, is not directly but indirectly related to the kid's problem. However disjointed the passages of a kid's life may be, they in fact all lead back to some central urging of his own. Image and analogy can be used to allow the kid to see his way more clearly through the tangle of conflicts that engulf him, so that he can hack out new, more practical and productive passages for himself.

5

COMMUNICATING IN THE FAMILY

*"When I was sixteen I thought my father was a
damn fool. When I became twenty-one, I was amazed
to find how much he had learned in five Years."*
Mark Twain

KIDS FUNCTION NOT ONLY AS A SINGLE UNIT
BUT ALSO AS A PART OF THE FAMILY SYSTEM.
Analogies can help the entire family make a positive
adjustment. To use analogies successfully with a whole
family, the analogy must be embedded in a family system
context. More often than not, families function like
systems, not like groups of separate individuals in some
loose confederation. **When a family is functioning like a
system, a change in any one member affects other
members of the group as well as the group as a whole.**

This chapter is written more from a counselor's view
point to help the reader see how getting kids to listen
sometimes requires that other family members acquire
more perspective. As families experience the normal
developmental crises, the way they communicate, relate,
and problem solve results in agreements, rules of behavior
and the playing of roles for the purpose of bringing
stability to the family.

For example it is fairly common with the coming of
adolescence for kids to refuse to put up with the same old

boundaries in the family. Kids can bring new ideas and values into the family, demanding that it alter its boundaries to include outside input. These new ideas can become stressors with the potential to drive the family apart. However, for the kid, it can be a functional process of individuating from the family. The family can choose to listen to the new ideas, letting the kid play the role of promotor of exciting discussions, or they can condescendingly point out that what he has to say is nothing new, thus placing the kid in the role of a dummy the family loves.

SEEING HOW TO PARENT

It is a well know fact that in adolescence many kids will refuse the authoritarian control that they had so willingly accepted only a short while earlier. They might begin to challenge their parents' opinions and views on everything from politics to parenting. This can precipitate arguments between parents over how to approach a kid. One of the parents, for example, might want to clamp down on a kid and demand that he continue to conform to the family rules. This parent might attempt to control the kid by refusing to allow him to see any of his friends. The other parent might think these measures too severe. While the pain that results from a process such as this is all too evident to the family, the underlying dynamics may remain invisible to the parents.

Through the use of analogy, the family is often able to see more clearly how to approach the problem. A way to begin is to use the metaphor of sea coast erosion. The family could discuss whether or not they feel that they can hold back the sea forever.

*The family might then relate its
situation to those who are attempting to
maintain the eroding coastline by building
bulkheads. The family might conclude
that it is similar to the National Park
Service, going through much experimentation
and frustration before discovering that
building bulkheads against the sea speeds
and intensifies the erosion instead of
retarding it.*

They could discuss how erosion is gentler where one accepts it as an inevitable reality rather than fights it. The family could explore ways to be cope with and be flexible with the new values of the kid, and allow the adolescent to gently discover his identity by taking excursions from the family and eventually leaving. Many families find that having an analogy for describing the process they are experiencing makes life less stressful when the clashes between members of the family occur.

Analogies alone are not sufficient for dealing with problems in family systems. The skilled user of analogies in families often becomes a student of how families function. A number of prominent writers on family therapy have explored in great detail the myriad possibilities that families may choose in dealing with stress to the family system (Bowen,1978; Halcy,1976; Minuchin,1974; Satire, 1972; and Palazzoli, 1978). This chapter provides strategies, many of which derive from the above bodies of work, for using analogies to work with issues of power, alliance and individuation in the family. **A strategy · that works well both for the construction and delivery of analogies for encouraging cooperation and a receptive attitude is the technique of reframing.** This technique is fundamental to all successful work with analogies in a family context.

REFRAMING

One of the main concerns of most families or parents is that they be seen as good. Palazzoli (1974) says that **kids can be very talented at making their parents appear in the worst possible light.** Palazzoli then suggests the "connotative technique" as the way to approach this problem. Using this reframing technique, the family interprets their actions toward the kid as indications of their best intentions for the kid.

For example the family might have a son who attempts to make the them appear as backward folks against whom he must act out as the only way to achieve any independence. The parents could reframe their actions as indicating a real insight into their son in that they know he doesn't appreciate his freedom and can't make good use of it unless he has to fight for it. Reframed in this way, the parents have been going overboard to help him.

It is also important to reframe the son's actions so that he can be seen as having good intentions. The boy could be seen by the parents as an explorer who wants everyone in the family to share his good experiences. Palazzoli has described this method as "the golden road for entering into the family system." It relaxes everyone about being good or bad persons by casting all participants in a good light.

Another way to go about describing the kid in positive terms would be to tell the story of someone who had problems very much like the young man's, and then go on to show how he became a hero. If the character in the analogy is a great hero, then one unspoken idea is that the adolescent in this family could become a hero also.

BEING A FAMILY

When the helpers of a troubled kid come to the point of being totally unable to even formulate a reason for why a kid would continue acting out without apparent reason, they might look at family dynamics.

It may be that the kid would rather be a problem than see a problem explode in his face.

He may realize, consciously or unconsciously that when he is a problem, his parents don't argue, fight or threaten divorce. That is, he protects them by giving them something to focus on rather than their own problem-ridden relationship. In many cases the kid also protects his own feelings. I have had many kids tell me how their stomachs "turn upside down" when their parents are arguing.

It may be that the kid has experienced intense rejection from one or both of his parents and is attempting to see if the parent will confirm acceptance and love by putting up with whatever the kid does. The kid could be making the parents prove themselves. In another case, the kid might be acting out the family's problems. Or the kid may be used by the parents to argue with each other. In this case, instead of fighting each other they displace their anger into a fight with the child. This way they can have their angry encounter and yet still form a coalition as husband and wife around the problem of how to help their kid who they are constantly having to correct.

Increasingly, single parent families are becoming more common. These families are vulnerable to several problems. One problem is that the single parent may begin to expect the kid to play the role of the missing spouse. While it makes sense to expect a kid to help the single parent by taking on extra chores, problems can result when the kid is expected to lend adult emotional support to his parent. Being presented with serious problems of adulthood that the kid is unprepared to handle can be emotionally upsetting.

A way to understand this is to imagine
yourself on a ship at sea in a storm.
What you want to hear from the captain
is that he's been through this before
and knows what to do. Everything's
going to be okay. If, on the other hand,
the captain started asking your opinion
of what to do or actually left control
of the ship up to you, how would you feel?

Another problem is that as the kid takes on adult responsibilities, he expects adult privileges. This can make the kid highly resistant to being told what to do by school staff or parents. I once heard a kid who had resolved this parental-child problem explain it metaphorically by saying that **he could stand in his father's shoes but he couldn't fill them.**

A good way to understand how stressful it can be for a kid to play the emotional role of an adult is to see the movie, *"Big"*. In this movie a kid is given his wish of being as big as an adult. He remains a kid in other ways and attempts to live in an adult world with a kid's emotional and social development. He enjoys his new power but is frightened.

A metaphorical way for attempting to explain this need the kid has to assert his power while fearing to take total control is to

Think of a builder who pushes against a new
wall he has constructed, and hopes he can push
very hard without it falling over.

TAKING CHARGE OF THE KID

Family problems can be very complex and difficult to understand and even more complicated to attempt to resolve in some helpful way for the kid. However, I have found that a common thread tends to run through most families of troubled kids. Where the family is troubled, the kid tends to see himself either as guilty, in some way, of helping to cause the trouble and needing to take some central responsibility for fixing it; or, sees himself as unfairly treated and thus justified in doing whatever he likes with regard to his family and others. With a few exceptions, it tends to be helpful to the kid if he views his family as properly in charge of him.

It has been my experience that a kid doesn't lose respect for the parents because the parents begin to take charge of the kid. A kid rather tends to respect parents who reduce his level of stress. A kid is far more likely to talk seriously about what's troubling him if he feels that his parents are skilled at getting things accomplished despite the kid's best attempts at preventing it. While the kid may attempt to run over his family, he would rather respect his family for providing him some wise counsel and secure boundaries as he tries to gain independence.

ADJUSTING FAMILY HIERARCHY

Up to this point we've been discussing ways that family members can become more sensitive to underlying family dynamics and to learn what is needed to improve family happiness. Any discussion of change in a family must eventually deal with the fact that the family itself must maintain the change. Often, maintaining gains depends on how power is discharged when stress appears. The family needs to become sensitive to who holds the power in the family and to learn how power is best used to promote family happiness.

To understand where the power is in the family is to understand family hierarchy. In some cases the normal hierarchy of parents in charge of the kid is reversed and for all practical purposes the kid controls the family. Analogies can help the family take charge of the kid where family hierarchy problems exist.

As Jay Haley (1980) has pointed out, reversals of

family hierarchy are one of the prime difficulties which a family often faces with a troubled kid. The kid often is in charge of the family rather than the other way around. Families sometimes allow this reversal in hierarchy to occur because somewhere they have decided that setting limits with the child will cause more anxiety which could lead to running away, suicide or some other dangerous problem, or at the least, a worsening of the kid's difficulties. Other reasons for hierarchy reversals are: (1) the family abdicates responsibility; (2) the family declares itself powerless; (3) the family in some conscious or unconscious way wants for the kid to remain a problem or at least not continue to grow emotionally and socially. One possible motive for the parents' desire to keep the kid from growing up is that they as a family do not want to have to begin to cope with their next developmental step, that of seeing their child differentiate from them and begin the process of leaving them, forcing the parents into a new stage of life, life without children.

The family needs to know that when a kid is in charge of a family, he is highly vulnerable to anxiety. This is because the kid with very little experience in the real world of adult decision making has to keep wondering what will happen to him next. Analogy can help bring home the point.

> *It's sort of like parking in a no parking zone. If you know full well you're going to be ticketed but decide to do it anyway, treating the ticket as a payment to a parking lot, then you won't feel anxious. However, if you're not really sure whether or not the policeman tickets people on that street and worry about whether or not he'll ticket you and what it will cost, then obviously you'll become anxious.*

In a family where the rules are clear and the family is in charge, carrying out the rules consistently, kids feel more secure. Once the kid knows the rules, he will have less anxiety even though he may not get his way as often, because he'll stop getting anxious over attempting to win his way.

However, in the case of family hierarchy as with most other issues of human relations,there are no absolutes. **It is not absolutely the case that in all matters the family should be in charge of the kid.** For example, the father might be a very successful workaholic who only spends time with the family when he is forced to by the kids acting out. It may be that some problem he's bothered by, such as overweight, can be used as an occasion for him to spend more time with his kid. In this case, the kid might need to be in charge of the father's weight loss. The kid might be in charge of seeing that his father goes running with him every morning. A good way to talk about this is to discuss the ways in which having a kid can benefit a father. Hopefully the father will conclude something positive such as, by having a kid, he is forced to enjoy some of his own youth by doing again with his kid some of the things he used to enjoy so much.

Incidentally, another good strategy for a parent to use in getting back in touch with his childhood is to share experiences out of his childhood with his spouse. For example, **each parent can remember something he or she liked to do as a child and teach it to each other.** Adults are often amazed to see how easy it is to get back into a childhood state of consciousness and to see how good it feels. For example, an adult can begin pretending he is nine years old and tell his wife how to play marbles just as he might have done with a friend when he was a kid. His wife might instruct him in playing jacks or some other game she would have told a friend about as a child. A lot of laughter usually results from reconnecting with our own childhood state of consciousness. Sometimes adults let their hair down a bit more. It can help the adult to better understand his children.

Another important concept is family alliances. The

case of Jane below illustrates how dysfunctional unhealthy family alliances can become.

PROMOTING HEALTHY FAMILY ALLIANCES

Jane: A Case of Unhealthy Family Unities - Forest Path Analogy

A classic family response to family stress is the alliance of family members against others within as well as outside family. Within the family, for example, a teenage girl may build an alliance with her mother against her father to obtain a particular end. For example, I once did therapy with a girl named Jane, her natural mother and her newly arrived stepfather. The girl was referred because of sexual acting out behavior and verbal aggression in the school. As it turned out, she had enticed her stepfather to make sexual overtures, which she then used for manipulating him. When he subsequently refused to be manipulated by her and attempted to father her, she then formed an alliance with her mother by telling her mother about her stepfather's sexual advances.

When I as counselor met with her, she very quickly attempted to form an alliance with me against her stepfather by saying that he had sexually abused her. In fact he had done nothing more than act friendly toward her. The girl's purpose was simply to drive her stepfather out of the home so that she could continue living with her mother in a sister-sister relationship. Under this arrangement, she was free to do most anything she wished. The trouble was that, with her system, she was failing school and miserably depressed.

In this girl's case, as in many families, the family system attempted to adapt to new pressures without changing its basic routines. To the degree the family tried to stay the same, crises developed in the face of the forces of change.

In the case of the girl cited above, a triangular relationship formed in which the girl became the victim, the stepfather the villain, and the mother the rescuer. The family members began talking in paradoxical ways to each other. The whole family decided to reduce some of the stress in the short run by drafting a set of home rules that all agreed on. However, after complete agreement that the rules were fair and useful, the girl accused her stepfather of being the villain again because he followed the rules too closely.

The girl was to lose a privilege if she did not call home when she expected to be late. She explained that she tried to call but the telephone ate all her money, and her stepfather shouldn't have taken away a privilege. The mother then entered an alliance with the girl explaining that she thought the stepfather would have been wiser to use discretion in this case. To all of which the stepfather responded that he was damned if he did and damned if he didn't. Furthermore, he pointed out that, if the agreement isn't followed exactly and exceptions are made, then the girl can just make up any story she likes and the agreement will mean nothing. The girl then said that the real problem was that her stepfather didn't trust her. Then the mother told the daughter she should respect her stepfather and not say mean things to him just because he didn't know what to do. Some of the paradoxical communications of the family in this case could be restated in the following way.

1) My stepfather violated the agreement by doing exactly what it said.

2) My daughter should respect her father even though he is too dumb to carry out the agreement wisely.

3) If I, the stepfather, follow the rules exactly, I will be just as wrong as if I don't do so.

The problem is that the family has difficulty finding a way to accept new possibilities. I first agreed with the stepfather that indeed he was in a dilemma. Then I informed the girl that her basic insight was accurate, in that some flexibility makes for easier acceptance of rules. And certainly, I told the mother, she was being responsible when she demanded that her daughter respect the stepfather. Then I told them that in their case:

Using a contract or agreement is like
making a trail through dense undergrowth.
At first you have to follow the way you
want to make it exactly, and till over time,
you learn the path well. Later, you will want
to be more flexible and be able to go off the
path knowing that it is easy to get back on track
anytime you want because the path is obvious.

GOING BEYOND GOOD INTENTIONS

I often help the family to see that each of them is very complicated with many parts wanting to go in many directions. I say that everyone is well intentioned but something more than good intentions is needed.

In this way, the family comes to view **any impulse which might produce guilt or low self-esteem** as simply **one part of the person attempting to have a say in how things are run.** In the example above each family member is reframed in a positive way: stepfather is in a dilemma; daughter has insight; and mother is a responsible parent. The conclusion is clear: the agreement will be followed to the letter until it is so well understood and the family so certain of its course, that it can allow for greater flexibility in being a family.

Family members need to interpret the actions of other family members not as attacks, insensitivity or ignorance but as idiosyncrasies of their personality makeup. The daughter lets her passion for insight get in her way. The mother lets her desire to be a good parent and protect her daughter get in the way. What reframing does is to enable the family to be objective about their confused feelings.

The use of the metaphor of the forest path needing to be well worn before the family members leave it is hard for anyone to argue with. In this case metaphor helps everyone to follow the rules.

Another serious problem for families is when the kid becomes too dependent upon a parent for the fulfillment of his psychological needs. In Terry's case below the mother has allowed herself to become too protective of Terry for his own good.

The father has for the most part left the parenting of Terry to the mother and has concentrated on working long hours as the bread winner for the family. In this case by becoming a problem at school Terry involves his father more in the family and brings him into the role of being supportive of his mother. In this way Terry's actions serve to protect the family by bringing them closer together. Unfortunately, this type of family protection is not in the best interest of Terry. While it encourages mom, dad and Terry to join in an alliance against the school, it is an alliance based on communication and problem solving that becomes ever more frustrating as it never succeeds in helping Terry to succeed in school.

DEPENDENCY PROBLEMS
Terry: A Case of Overdependence on a Parent - Biblical Analogies

Terry is a case in which the parenting of the child was left almost entirely to one parent. In Terry's case, it was his mother. Terry's mother was a depressed lady who took pride in the fact that she had almost single-handedly brought up Terry as a fine child. However, when Terry reached adolescence, he shocked her by getting kicked out of school frequently. Terry told his mother that the school had it in for him, because, as she could see, he was no worse than his friends who had

91

not been thrown out. His mother bought the argument, as she didn't want to believe her son was bad or that she had failed as a parent. As a result of some earlier family problems, she felt some guilt for not having been a stronger wife and parent. She desperately needed to be a success with her son and made their relationship the central focus of her life.

As Terry proceeded into adolescence, the mother observed:

1) Terry was no longer as happily compliant at school or home.

2) Terry angrily attacked her on occasions for making him do things he really didn't want to do.

3) He blamed mother and father for his past mistakes citing poor parenting.

4) He demanded more freedom.

5) He lied about things that happened. In fact, he even stole money and said a robber got it.

6) He attempted to get her to side with him whenever others were confronting him. During these periods, he seemed exactly like the old Terry she had known.

Terry's mom had found much peace through religion. One of her first courses of action was to recommend that the pastor intervene with Terry. However, soon Terry refused to see the pastor. This occurred after the pastor visited the school and found that Terry really did have some problems that needed to be addressed. Terry and his family then began to slip into the following eight part cycle with the school.

1) Terry acts out when not allowed to do exactly what he wants by staff or another student.

2)   Terry accepts responsibility for his actions
        in crisis intervention sessions with school staff,
        but then changes his story when he gets home.

3)   At home, Terry cries and tells mother that the
        reason he had difficulty at school was because the
        staff is biased toward him.

4)   Mother goes to the school and attacks the staff
        for being biased against her son and for running a
        program that is cold and disciplined rather than
        loving and spiritual.

5)   Terry cries in front of mother and
        school staff when confronted with the truth. He
        admits he did something wrong but that it was
        because of the way the staff was treating him.

6)   Mother joins Terry in crying and admits that both
        she and Terry have some problems, but that the
        school program will never succeed, and that no one
        knows how to help her son.

7)   Mother goes home and tells father that she met
        with school staff and can see that they are
        against Terry and are not going to help him.

8)   Father visits school, angrily wanting to know what
        is going on there. He finally determines that the
        school is accurate about its interventions with
        Terry and mother, but he thinks mother might be
        right in not believing that the school program can
        succeed.

        The school counselor got the family to agree that
they were going to solve their problem rather than
attempt to change the context somehow by placing the
kid in a different school. The strategy was to get
agreement from mom and dad that dad would take over
sole responsibility for parenting Terry. Mom would act

as a consultant to dad but cease to take the active parenting role with regard to discipline. Dad would make decisions about the kid's privileges. Dad would meet with school officials when necessary. Mom's decision was seen as the ultimate heroic act of stepping out of the active parenting role for a brief time to allow Terry the opportunity to have a strong male role model and the opportunity to build a sense of his own identity. Later, it was explained he would once again be able to have a close relationship with his mother.

The story of the young Indian braves who must go off by themselves when they come of age and find a new name for themselves was used. It was pointed out that it just seemed natural that a young Indian needed to leave the women for a while and build a new identity and relationship with the men of the tribe. When he returned, he could again have close relationships; but they would be as a strong, upstanding young man who could provide protection and support for the family rather than as a child dependent on the family for protection.

While the mother agreed to this arrangement, Terry tried desperately to manipulate her into her old role. She would likely have fallen back into it, if the counselor had not used frequent family sessions and supportive communication to keep mother strong. In this case, the counselor used biblical analogies because both parents were so deeply committed to living their lives by *The Bible.* The counselor was speaking to them in a language they had already learned, tapping a source they had faith in. I should note in passing that it was not necessary for the counselor to hold identical beliefs on a literal level. It was sufficient for the counselor to respect their metaphorical value. Here are a few examples of how the family's personal source of wisdom was tapped.

1) The Counselor and family discussed how the Devil tempts the mother to break her resolution and give into evil by using her son to manipulate her. All parties

agreed to fight the Devil at all costs.

2) The family discussed the incident when Jesus found the money lenders in the temple. The point here was to see that Jesus did not bargain or attempt to be soft on the money lenders. He swiftly kicked them out of his Father's house, saying that they had violated the rules of his Father's house.

3) The family discussed how desperate the Devil might get in working through their son. He might even have the son refusing to go to church for example, but that they nevertheless should hold firm.

4) The counselor discussed with mother the idea of self-sacrifice. She pointed out that God never meant by self-sacrifice that parents should give the child whatever he wanted but rather that self-sacrifice meant enduring the pain of parenting.

5) The counselor discussed with mom how she could model Christ's behavior by being more assertive. The counselor pointed out that Christ could be meek and loving rather than mean and angry, but that he nevertheless always acted on the principles he believed in.

6) The family discussed how the prophets in the *Bible* never expected a life without pain. They talked about the good that waited for those who truly acted wisely.

7) They discussed how Noah was not able to save everyone. The counselor pointed out that despite all her attempts, the mother might not be able to save her son, but that would not make her a bad mother if she did everything she could.

8) In working with the family, the father was told about the Medieval play called *The Deluge* in which

Noah has to push his wife into the ark because she refuses to board it.

9) The counselor pointed out that Noah on one occasion was discovered drunk by one of his sons, Ham, and the son was punished for making a spectacle of Noah. The idea was that Noah's drinking problem did not reflect on his wisdom in following God's advice, building the ark and directing his family appropriately.

10) The Counselor discussed with the husband and wife the story of the Jews wandering in the wilderness and how this is sort of the way an adolescent finds himself.

Of course, there is almost no end to the variety of religious stories that can be helpful with the right family. These stories in fact, were surely written down, not just to record events but also because they serve to lead man out of the darkness in which he sometimes finds himself.

Finally, Terry's counselor had to help his family prepare for their son's success. As Terry became more self-confident and secure, he made friends, built a sense of who he was and finally stopped acting out at school. It was a real problem keeping the family from attempting to find some imperfection in Terry so that they could go on working on the rewarding enterprise of helping Terry.

Letting go of Terry as the problem could only result in the family having to deal with their own marital problems. It is often a very tough step for parents to make to learn how to communicate in such a way that they keep their relationship positive while addressing their problems. Often well entrenched resentments and old hurts rear their heads. Even here the stories of Job and others can be helpful.

The counselor and Terry's family agreed that the launching of Terry as a young man with his own identity had been a success that no one could take away from them. They agreed that, with the same seriousness and dedication, they could now solve almost any problem.

I have found 30 communication guidelines to be very helpful for families to use in establishing a unified focus on the particular problem at hand.

THIRTY FAMILY COMMUNICATION GUIDELINES

1) **Begin work on the least threatening of topics.**

2) **Have parents list behaviors of the kid that concern them.** Parents list exactly how they reward or punish the kid's behaviors. This allows all to understand what has worked and what hasn't

3) **Don't try things that have failed.**

4) **Attempt solutions that have high probability for success.** Parenting is a long and difficult process, particularly if the children are a handful. If one is to continue to be motivated as a parent to do the hard work that's necessary to help children change, then the parent needs to be able to succeed.

5) **Use behavioral contracts.** with multiple copies of what the family agrees to do. The family can then sit down to talk about their problems and be perfectly clear about where they are headed and what they decided in a previous meeting.

6) **Address feelings of guilt.** All family members need to be clear that no one has failed as a person, because things in the family are not working as well as everyone would like.

7) **Don't get discouraged.**

8) **Listen to all the children in the family.** Sometimes another child has a clear understanding of what's

happening in the family.

9) <u>List all the stresses in the family.</u> Be certain to look at perceived stress, not just obvious stressors.

10) <u>Get all family members to agree on what is the problem</u>. No point in simply hoping everyone is working on the same problem.

11. <u>Give the problem kid tasks that support the well being of the family.</u>

12) <u>Encourage family members to learn to laugh at themselves.</u>

13) <u>Encourage family members to look to the future rather than the past.</u> The main goal most of the time is to discuss how to bring about the desired end in the future not how to understand the past.

14) <u>Get the family to focus all of its power on the fulfillment of a task.</u> When a family works together with a single purpose, they are often amazed at what they can accomplish.

15) <u>Encourage family members to become sensitive to the roles each assigns to other family members.</u> The kid's problem may be that he is stuck with a role he desperately needs to get out of.

16) <u>Be sure that family members are careful not to be outwardly hostile to another family member.</u>

17) <u>Be aware that anyone who seriously problem solves with the family becomes a part of the family.</u>

18) <u>Work to see that family members become sensitive to what they do to each other.</u>

19) <u>Have family members read books and articles on</u>

human development to better understand each other.

20) **Make family members aware that they should expect stress when anyone enters or exits the family.**

21) **Find positive things to say about the kid.**

22) **The family as a whole questions its irrational beliefs.** Family members can get upset with each other because of what they erroneously believe society, friends, or other family members think or expect.

23) **Check if the kid is trying to gain love by proving himself.** Family members give unconditional love.

24) **Discuss issues of assertiveness.** Do family members really do what they want and need to do?

25) **Look for ways that family members set each other up for trouble.** Do members pull each other's strings?

26) **Observe to what degree the kid's problem is a problem of family communication.**

27) **Discuss how adolescence opens the family up to new and different ideas and values.**

28) **Check if the family is more upset with the manner of the kid or with what he actually does or says.**

29) **Discuss the phrase "blood is thicker than water."** These types of phrases can be motivating.

30) **Discuss whether love is really enough.**

The 30 guidelines help families function better but they don't directly enable the family to achieve its over-all goal of being happy. I have found the following ten strategies to be tasks families can do to actively promote happiness.

10 STRATEGIES FOR FAMILY HAPPINESS

1)   _Discuss change._ The family commits itself to change by discussing what lies ahead if the kid changes.

2)   _Project the kid's life into the future._ Talk about how fast the future comes and if the kid makes it, how he will parent his own children.

3)   _Have some adult talk._ Recognize the importance of the parents in the home talking on a regular basis about decision making.

4)   _Have some adult fun._ Parents take time for quality experiences with each other. Aside from the joy having fun produces, it also sends a message to the children that parents don't exist just to support the kids in the home.

5)   _Shake up the balance._ Make a conscious effort to breakup unhealthy alliances.

6)   _Do fourteen minute writing._ One family member writes down verbatim what the other family member is saying about the good and bad things that have been happening. Then the other member takes his turn. When one writes down what another says, it's clear he heard.

7)   _Do wishful thinking._ Talk about how good things could be. Wishful thinking can create positive mutual expectations and goals among family members.

8)   _Travel in the happy past._ Family members share the wonderful earlier times when things seemed to be going great.

9)   _Have a week of fun._ The family agrees to have a week of fun at all costs.This helps to break the painfully dysfunctional cycle a family has been going through.

10)   _Plan surprises._ Each family member takes on the task of providing the rest of the family with a surprise fun activity.

ANALOGIES FOR PARENTING

The following analogies can be adapted to individual family circumstances. The first rule for which an analogy is useful is that if a family is to be able to communicate in a helping way with a kid, the family needs to help itself first. I'm reminded of the instructions we are given at the beginning of an airplane flight about using the oxygen masks. They tell us, "When the oxygen masks drop down, put one on yourself first, then on your child."

The Baby Birds
Family Says: "The kids aren't ready."
Sometimes baby birds have to be pushed out of the nest in order to learn how to fly.
DISCUSSION: When will your children be ready? How will you know? Do you think you'll have to do any pushing? How do you think it would be best to do the pushing?
       *   *   *   *   *

Catching Up
Family Says: "He's getting behind."
I myself didn't graduate from high school until I was 19, and I have not found that it harmed me in anyway.
Einstein had to leave school his senior year for 6 months on a psychiatric discharge because he was having difficulties. Did he get behind? Buckminster Fuller, the engineering genius of the geodesic dome among other things, wandered a lot of roads to find things out for himself? Did he get behind by dropping out of college? Thomas Edison, a problem child, was pulled out of school and educated by his mom. Did he get behind? Many

Americans had their education interrupted by World War II, but when they returned found their education all the more rewarding and enriched by the depth of experience they brought to it. Time doing something else isn't necessarily wasted.

DISCUSSION: Who has set the clock? What is the standard the kid is racing against? What does it mean to get behind? Behind what, whom?

* * * * * *

Learning The Hard Way

Family Says: "He has to learn everything the hard way."

Have you heard of the school of hard knocks? How many kids have learned to keep away from hot stoves or camp fires without ever getting burned? Learning is a matter of style. When you learn something the hard way, do you ever forget it?

DISCUSSION: What's wrong with learning things the hard way? Is there any way to safeguard against it?

* * * * * *

Single Parenting

Family Says: "I'm probably making a lot of big mistakes trying to parent all by myself."

Imagine having to suddenly switch from driving a compact car to driving an 18 wheel tractor trailer with no practice at all.

One thing about single parenting is that it usually comes about very suddenly. A single parent has little practice with being a single parent before the job is thrust upon him. How do you expect most people would do at an extremely complex task for which they had no training or practice?

DISCUSSION: Talk about one's expectations of how a parent should perform. Which expectations are reasonable? Does the parent expect to be a perfect parent, and is there really any such thing? In fact, are the people who write books on good parenting perfect parents themselves?

* * * * * *

A Place in Heaven
Family Says: "It's tough being a single parent."

You know, for the kinds of troubles you're dealing with I'm sure there's a place in heaven prepared for you. Ever try moving a thick 4 x 8 foot piece of plywood by yourself?
DISCUSSION: How is this parent like Mother Theresa or Albert Schweitzer in the sense that the parent is doing the job that two people or more ought to be doing? Talk about putting up an 8 foot fence by yourself with no one to hold things up while you nail or folding a sheet with no one to hold up the other end.

* * * * * *

When They Are Twenty-five
Parent Says: "They think he's great and I'm an ogre."

Your pet definitely does not appreciate your taking him for a rabies shot but is that any reason to stop?

It may be that your children will not fully appreciate you until they have children themselves. Maybe when they are 25 or so. Or even later.
DISCUSSION: Discuss how natural it is to take for granted what you have and to build fantasies about what you don't have.

* * * * * *

Abuse
Mother Says: "I let his father treat us bad so I don't deserve respect."

Have you ever noticed how people who are kidnapped

talk about building a special relationship with the kidnapper that enabled them to get along until they could get free?

You're free enough now to know what you need to do with people who treat you badly. Before you were not so strong, and you did what you thought was best. In fact, whether for good or bad, probably if you hadn't supported this man while he was treating you poorly, he might not have made it as long as he did. It sounds as though he must have been pretty insecure to treat you so badly. It may be that even, in spite of the bad he did to you, that you, being compassionate, couldn't do anything other than to help him, at least for a while in his time of need. Would you really judge another person as having failed because he was compassionate?

DISCUSSION: No matter how bad the past might have been, do you think the past has to continue to influence your child now that you've become strong? What will happen if you and your child stop practicing the kinds of things that went on in the past and begin practicing the new things that you know you need to do now that you're strong?

* * * * * *

PUNISHMENT

Family Says: "I don't believe in punishment. Jesus preached love."

It's true Jesus preached love, but let me ask you, what did He do when He found the moneylenders in the temple violating His Father's rules for how to act in His Father's House?

DISCUSSION: Does love mean allowing someone to break rules and do anything he wants? Is it contradictory to have certain boundaries while you attempt to give a kid all the love you can? Are you really loving anyone if you let him destroy his life?

* * * * * *

Questioning The Rules

Family Says: "The kids are always questioning my rules."

You know when you're building a new house you often go around and push on the wall, just to see how strong it is. How would you feel if you pushed on the wall and it fell over?

DISCUSSION: Children are going to push against our rules and regulations just to see that they're strong. It's not our job to cave in and fall over. It's our job to reassure them, in a spirit of love and respect, that we are strong.

* * * * * *

Blueprint

Family Says: "We're always arguing about what it was we agreed on."

If you're going to build a house, isn't it important to have a blueprint?

DISCUSSION: Discuss what agreed upon means. Does it need to be written down?

* * * * * *

The Racecar Driver

Family Says: "My kid always blames the unexpected actions of others or something I did for preventing him from completing a task."

If you were in an auto race, would you be able to focus entirely on your own driving without adjusting for the other drivers skidding or cutting in front of you?

DISCUSSION: Once you've established the metaphor of racecar driving, you can go back to the kid and say, "Hey, did you have another wreck in the race?" Sort of make it into a joke, but a serious one.

* * * * * *

Toothpaste

Family Says: "If he would only do what I say, he wouldn't get in such bad situations."

Maybe you should say to him, once the toothpaste is out of the tube, it's hard to get back into the tube.

DISCUSSION: You can say, "Oops, looks like the toothpaste is out again."

*   *   *   *   *   *

The Hostages

Family Says: "He says we are unfair."

You know that he probably feels exactly the way hostages do. And you might say to him, "You know if you were in an airplane and were taken hostage you would think it very unfair. But right after you finish telling yourself how unfair it is, you'd then be faced with another concern. What do you think that would be?"

DISCUSSION: Kids enjoy such discussions. They enjoy fantasizing about how to save their lives in dangerous situations. These fantasies can then be related back to the situation at hand.

*   *   *   *   *   *

Pampered Pet

Family says: "Growing up is tough today."

What would happen to the pampered house cat if he had to survive on his own?

DISCUSSION: You have no doubt seen documentaries of animals such as the lioness in *Born Free*, who have been brought up as pets and then have to be released into the wild by their caretakers. Preparing the animal to survive in the tough world outside has to be a carefully planned process.

*   *   *   *   *   *

Letter Writing

Family member says, "He won't stop interrupting long enough to hear what I'm trying to say."

What would happen if you wrote him a letter?

DISCUSSION: How easy is it to interrupt someone when you are reading their letter?

CONCLUSION: Kids bring new ways of doing things into the family. These ideas can be particularly stressful for the parents. They can drive the family apart. A classic response to family stress is for family members to build alliances with each other against other family members or outsiders depending upon the perceived source of the threat. The alliance can be unhealthy. The alliance can isolate a family member or it can become the vantage point from which one family member manipulates the rest of the family.

Family dynamics can be very complex and difficult to see, much less understand. Analogies can cut through the tangle of confusion around family issues.

6

COMMUNICATING IN A CRISIS

"An idea like a stone wedged in a delicate machine can arrest one's whole process of physic interaction and spontaneous growth."
                                        --D. H.Lawrence

A KID'S SOLUTION TO HIS PROBLEMS CAN LEAD TO GREATER PROBLEMS.
   A poor solution to a problem can become a basic cause of stress. The Eastern philosophers call this process karma. It is a situation in which the attempt to control one thing requires the person to control other things. For a kid, practically any issue can become a control issue: When the parent asks him to remove his hat or coat; when the teacher asks him to sit in a different place; when the parent doesn't allow him to leave the house; when the teacher attempts to help him against his will; or when the teacher doesn't help him at the moment he desires it. The kid may throw a tantrum, run out of the room, throw something, clam up and refuse to do anything, or do some other bizarre act. A kid's attempt to control any of these situations can lead to a crisis. Once the kid makes the wrong move, he then finds himself with an even more difficult problem to solve.
   Another side of this problem is the kid who is able to

avoid dealing with most crises in life and so never learns the skills which come from working through crises. This type of kid may encounter trouble later when he can't get what he needs by avoiding conflict any longer. Since all new developmental phases require change and adjustment and since success in handing one phase seems to promote success in handing the next phase, it is difficult to progress though life by avoiding or being protected from threats.

What constitutes a crisis? Is it a life threatening situation or what? The answer is that any inability to cope can produce a crisis. As Gerald Caplan has said, "Crisis refers to one's emotional reaction, not to the threatening event itself." If a kid thinks he needs more control of a situation and can't get it, he is in crisis.

The Eastern sages have a solution for crisis. They call it nirvana. Nirvana simply means a peaceful nonstressed state of mind resulting from letting go of the need to be godlike and control things. How often have I heard parents say, **"If my kid would just let go and try to cooperate a little!"** The problem with getting a kid in crisis to just let go and flow with things is the same as with any other persons under stress. He honestly believes that if he gives up what control he has, he'll be in even worse shape. It's the same problem one faces in attempting to help a drowning swimmer.

Furthermore, kids in crisis want a quick fix. It's like Brer Rabbit and the Tar-Baby. Once he gets one paw stuck by an emotional reaction, rather than carefully thinking out a solution, he quickly commits a second emotional act to attempt to extricate himself. Thus begins the vicious cycle in which each new attempt at problem solving leads to a greater problem.

WORKING THROUGH A CRISIS

John: Case of a Stressed Out kid - Black Belt Analogy

I once counseled a young man named John who was heavily stressed by events in his family. First his father had deserted the family, then his mother had given him to an uncle. He didn't get consistent parenting and became very frustrated trying to get along on the streets. He was basically a gentle kid who would try to communicate in a macho way to impress other boys; and then, when they carried the macho game to a physical level, he had to fight. He was a rather large red haired boy, a bit overweight, with fair skin and freckles. If you didn't know better, you'd expect him to be a scholar and maybe a teacher's pet. So it was difficult for him to make himself believable as a tough guy. He did come to be a good fighter though, and he also came to be the kind of kid who would lose control of himself at the slightest hint of criticism from another kid or adult.

The first stage for helping John was to get him to practice relaxation. John was not willing to sit still. If he wasn't out of control, he was trying to be macho; and if he was out of control, he couldn't sit still. When he lost control, John became flushed and shook as though he were having a seizure.

To help John while he was in a crisis, I first I had to get him to practice progressive muscle relaxation. He refused to do it because he was out of control. So I'd tell him the best way to learn how to fight better was to do like the karate experts and develop total control of his body. Then quickly I'd tell him to sit down and make a fist. He was already tensing his fist, so I was just going with his reactions. John would vehemently protest that deep muscle relaxation wasn't going to make him calmer because nothing would work when he was out of control. I'd tell him that as long as he was out of control he could practice becoming a better fighter.

He'd sit down, protesting all the while and make a fist. Then after about five seconds of his tensing his fist, I'd tell him to relax the fist. He'd do it. Then I'd have him alternately tense and relax one muscle after another until he had covered approximately twelve to 16 muscle groups. They include: hands, biceps, forehead, center face, lower face, neck, back, chest, abdomen, thigh, calf and foot. In between tensing and relaxing John, I provided patter such as, "You are calm, confident and secure, gaining ever more control over your body and learning the distinction between tension and relaxation." There is an excellent book and video tape by Bernstein and Borkovick(1973) on how to do the deep muscle relaxation, I was using.

John would often become as relaxed as a sleepy bear on a warm summer afternoon. Once John was calm, he and I could problem solve around his crisis. Also we worked at controlling his anger by getting John to become aware of the things he told himself that jacked up his anger. For example, John would say, "Nobody treats me like that and gets away with it." We then would come up with a phrase that John could say to himself to help preempt tantrums. For example we'd have John say to himself,

Like a black belt, I can take control of my body.

Helping a kid like John learn to relax requires the helper to learn how to relate to him in such a way that he'll try something he doesn't believe in such as progressive relaxation. It requires persistent attempts to build an ongoing dialogue with the kid at times when he is not so upset.

When it is done well, helping involves listening intently to the kid's story which he tells in little bits and pieces from time to time. Then you must find or invent a metaphor, that you can use as the focal point of your discussions with him. Like a flag carried into battle, it will serve as an inspiration and a reminder of the ideas and values it embodies. This dialogue requires skill both for intervening in crises as well as for using metaphor.

KEYS TO GOOD CRISIS WORK

The things to listen for in the discussions with the kid either before or during crisis intervention are the same as if you were looking for the crucial parts of any good story.

Does his story have a beginning, middle and a future that he can describe?

Does he have a good sense of where he's been and where he is headed?

What have been the traumatic events of his life?

What are the main problems that he's dealing with at the moment?

Does he string together various events and feelings from the past so that if someone says the wrong thing, pulls the wrong cord, the kid reacts emotionally as though the full complement of his problems are being experienced all at once at that moment?

For example, if he saw his father treated unfairly, does he reexperience that intensely every time he is mistreated. What resentments, traumas and experiences or unfairness in his life has he strung together? How do events in his life act symbolically to set him off? At what points does he speak of success, rejection or acceptance? Do we hear confusion, fear, anxiety, helplessness, frustration, threat, conflict or joy? In what ways is he rigid and in what ways flexible? How impulsive are the heroes and other characters of his stories? How high and how low are his expectations? Does he approve of himself? To what degree is he confronting reality honestly, and to what degree attempting to hide from it? What are his social relationships? Who does he include in his stories? Does he have any folk wisdom he falls back on in times of crisis? Will it be possible to give him any? What dysfunctional modes of thinking does he use? What are his defenses? What are his coping devices?

ANALOGIES AND DECISION MAKING

Be prepared to give the kid in crisis at least one little analogy that will serve him as a handle on his control over himself even if it is a general one. For example, with almost any kid who is upset, you can say,

*We are like tea bags. We don't know
our strength until we are in hot water.*

In addition to the basic information on the kid, it can be useful to you to know a little about his specific interests when you come to making up or choosing analogies and metaphors for him. We have been discussing how kids tangle up the events of their lives. Analogies give kids the opportunity to step outside the tangle and look at themselves.. Analogies teach kids to listen to how they are saying something as they are saying it.

Analogies allow us to suspend the habitual ongoing dialogue we have with ourselves about our day to day worries and expectations. Analogies, then, are powerful tools to use in crisis intervention when the helper is attempting to enable the kid to step back from the brink, and have a fresh look around at the landscape. The one thing that's usually true of all people in crisis is that a lot of stressors have closed around him at the same time leaving the kid with tunnel vision. Kids in crisis tend to edit out many possibilities. One way to use this concept of both being in the story as the participant and being outside the story as the storyteller is to say to the person:

*There is the upset part of you and
the sensible part of you. The sensible
part must now help the upset part.*

This kind of statement is useful after the kid has had an opportunity to ventilate and to describe the ongoing story of his problem. It is a way of bringing him back to the idea that he is now going to have to solve his problem. It tells the kid that he is going to have to be part of the solution. It is a good opportunity for the kid to look at the degree to which he is going to be able to use the sensible part of himself as opposed to the upset part. There are cases where it is not possible. The upset part just continues to be in sole control. That's a kind of situation in which you need to think about a more highly structured environment. But in most cases, kids are able to acknowledge the sensible part of themselves once it as been framed in that way.

Another way to get at this is to say to the person:

> *If we should trade chairs and you were the*
> *helper what would you have learned so far?*

While this process is going on, if the kid begins to slip back into the upset part of himself and says things that are not very functional, you can say to him,

> *You don't have to be so helpless, the*
> *sensible part of you is still very strong.*

Asking the kid to focus on the sensible part of himself optimizes learning conditions when the kid under stress. It reminds him to refocus on his goal rather than the obstacles in his way.

Another way to support the kid under stress is to let him know that his solution to the problem at hand doesn't have to be ideal. Leo Bellak tells a wonderful little tale I'll call *Bellak's Porcupine Tale*, which points up that a close approximation to the goal is sometime solution enough. My paraphrase of his story goes like this:

> *On a cold winter night a group of*
> *porcupines decided to move together to*
> *keep each other warm but ended up by hurting*
> *each other. So they moved apart, and*
> *they became very cold. Finally they*
> *found the optimum distance to help keep*
> *warm with the least hurt.*

In a crisis a kid doesn't have to find the perfect solution to his life problems. He can decide to work on a first task to begin to alleviate some of the pain and stress. *The Porcupine tale* makes a statement about adjustment in human relationships which is frequently an issue in crises.

FINDING A FOCUS AND MOVING ON

There comes a point in a crisis intervention, when the issue of movement has to be discussed. How are things going to change? What is the kid actually going to do about his situation?

This brings up a number of problems. It brings us back to motivation and to the reason why the kid is in trouble. Asking what the kid is actually going to do to change things, can cause the kid to become defensive and oppositional. This point can easily take us right back to where we started, with the kid wanting to replay the old upset feelings of anger or depression, wanting to ventilate. **It is important at this point to be able to say,**

> *We've been down this road before,*
> *and now we're at a crossroads where*
> *we could choose a different direction.*
> *Are we going to get stuck in the same*
> *old hole?*

The process of getting unstuck is a process of getting the kid to focus on a goal and go for it like a man swimming for the beach with a shark on his tail. People in crisis tend to try to avoid a central focus. They flounder around. They have tunnel vision and scream about the problem, but in fact, avoid what they need to do. It is interesting that the German word for depression is *"terschel,"* which actually means deception. A big part of the process in getting kids to move on is to get them to avoid deceiving themselves into not acting. Frequently during this phase, kids will say that they are

right and aren't going to change what they are doing. I
sometimes quote William James to kids at this point,

Even if you are on the right
track, you might get run over
if you are standing still.

It's important that one not think of this phase of
crisis intervention as just a trial and error phase in which
one simply tries anything and everything. This is the
point where one acts on his best judgement however
flawed. In this phase, what is needed is good problem
solving skills and good analogy making skills. The task is
to create a plausible story that could happen which would
produce a positive future in the kid's life. I often try to
get the kid thinking about how a great person or one of
his own heroes might cope. I also let him know that much
of our best learning comes from failure, so that either
way he goes, if he keeps his head about him, he's likely to
get stronger.

IDENTIFYING WITH HEROES

A good way to get a kid thinking in these terms is to
mention to him how Einstein used to problem solve since
kids believe Einstein was the greatest mind ever.
Einstein said the essence of his problem solving was
that he didn't let his own past knowledge get in the way
of finding solutions to problems. He didn't reason
himself out of going down a certain path because he was
already sure of where it would lead. In fact, Einstein
modestly talked about not knowing enough to deceive
himself. This way he was able to wander down paths more
knowledgeable men might have had too much sense to
pursue. The point here is not that the kid in crisis should
do anything that comes to mind but that he should keep
an open mind.
I often tell kids that Einstein used to stay cool and
consider many possibilities but that he could take action

when he needed to. Then I tell them the story of when Einstein caught a robber in his home, disarmed him and chased him away. In this way, I keep the kid interested with a true action story from Einstein's life, while I suggest that the kid model his problem solving on Einstein's. Of course, in helping a kid you might use some character other than Einstein; but it needs to be someone who is well known to the kid.

I also tell kids how Einstein had difficulties in school. His seventh grade teacher asked that he leave the school. During his senior year, he took a six month absence for "psychiatric" reasons. I let them know that even later when he was famous, he once took off his coat in a lecture he was giving only to find the audience laughing because he hadn't worn a shirt. This is just to let kids know that Einstein was human and could do some dumb things like them. In doing good crisis intervention with kids, building a bank of fascinating biographical tales can be very helpful.

Some kids go for athletes or movie stars as models. It really doesn't matter who the model is just so long as his life is sufficiently broad and deep to enable the kid to find answers to his problems. I have found that most kids are looking for heroes; and they'll take what you have to offer if the story is engaging.

You can, also make up a hero who is not famous but someone you say that you once met. Kids also like to think that they know someone who knew someone interesting. This hero can be the vehicle for a dialogue with the kid, a kind of go-between who carries messages about more functional ways to cope. It's good to keep heroic tales from newspapers available like the one I have in my office of the girl who was labeled retarded, sent to a juvenile corrections program, and later graduated at the top of her medical school class. I also have a newspaper story of an athlete I once helped, who had been in serious trouble with the law but later studied criminal justice in college.

These kinds of stories let kids know without a doubt that no matter how bad things may seem at any given time, there is always the possibility of making things better if the kid will just get moving and do something. I once met a parent who said that she pinned up little sayings and success stories around her house just so that her kids would have some good models to think about. She said, she was amazed to see that her kid's friends always looked forward to reading the sayings when they came to visit and always asked her about them.

I keep Van Gogh's awkward early drawing of a carpenter around so that when kid's ask who did that, I can say Vincent Van Gogh. They often reply that it looks like something anyone could do. I agree. I also show them some of the famous paintings of Cezanne, and then I let them know that he was an awful painter at first, but that because he was willing to try lots of things, rather than follow convention, he ended up a great painter, not just a good one.

FINDING THE RIGHT STATE OF MIND

Don Meichenbaum uses the image of a turtle to get young children to model staying cool and focusing on problem solving. He tells young children to think about what the turtle does when he is stumped. The turtle pulls his arms, legs and head inside his shell and problem solves.

One way to go about it with older kids is to have the kid close his eyes and visualize a situation similar to his own but different. The kid might create a situation somewhat different that has the same elements in it as his problem. He can then imagine a positive ending to the story. Crafting an ending to a story similar to his own can be the first step for a kid to take in solving his own problem. Once a kid arrives at a first step in solving his problem, he often can take it from there. As the Oriental proverb goes,

The first step is half the journey.

At some point you might want to talk to the kid about how anxiety works. It might be helpful for him to know how he can get himself upset by the things he tells himself. For example, you might point out to him a secret that speech makers have learned about anxiety. Speech makers know that when they see someone getting up in the back of the room and leaving, it is important not to catastrophize about it. For example, I tell the kid, if a speaker says to himself, "Oh my God, I'm so boring people are leaving," then he will get very anxious. In fact, the speaker will start making other mistakes and give a poor speech. But, if he says to himself, "Too bad that poor guy has to leave, he's going to miss the best lecture of his life," then the speaker remains cool. His speech is likely to be better delivered and received if he is less anxious in the way he talks to himself.

The kid needs to see that his own imagination is a very powerful force in determining how he reacts in crisis. While in some cases, by acts of will, he may be able to force himself to do things despite what he is imagining, this is not usually the case when a kid is under a lot of stress. I try to get the kid to appreciate the power of his imagination and to get him to start using it rather than fighting it. I tell him that he needs to say to himself, "I am going to be in the right state of mind."

A good story I have found to use in making kids sensitive to how powerful the imagination can be in helping them overcome problems is to tell them about the way athletes at the Olympics handle stress. I describe how they find the right state of mind. I explain that at the Olympics all of the athletes are great, and they know that even the slightest edge can make all the difference in the world. Therefore, many of the successful ones practice visualization. That is, these athletes practice seeing themselves succeed at the task before they attempt to do it. A great high jumper for example will "see" himself going over the bar. I also point out to them that the great athletes keep the image in their minds right up to the point that they do the task. Once he has come up with a good image for avoiding stress in the future, he needs to keep the solution before him and really make use of it.

Engaging a kid's imagination for focusing on problems in his life is often the key to helping him change. The real key then to crisis intervention is for the helper to be imaginative and encourage the same process in the kid. A side effect of using stories of heroes is that the kid will get the unspoken message that you must believe in him if you talk about him solving his problems the way great men have. And I believe the truth is that much of the success of the helper flows from the helper's deep belief that a kid, no matter how screwed up, could indeed become a great person. For this purpose, the helper himself needs models of people who overcame great adversity.

I always assume that every kid is one of the "superkids" Maya Pines describes in a *Psychology Today*(1979) article. She describes research being done on children who thrive in difficult situations. Maya Pines says, there are kids who "Whatever their circumstances--they may be the offspring of schizophrenics or children who are abused, extremely poor, or otherwise at risk--they respond to stress by developing extraordinary competence." As an example, I show kids the following news article, which I referred to earlier, from *USA Today*,

> *New doctor was once labeled 'retarded.'*
> *Albany, N.Y. -*
> *Mary Groda was the star of the graduating*
> *class at Albany Medical College on Thursday.*
> *A seasonal farm worker in Texas, she was*
> *illiterate at 16, an unwed mother at 18 and was*
> *labeled retarded at a reform school. Now the 35*
> *year old mother of two teenage children is a doctor*
> *and earned four awards for her work with*
> *patients.... She credits a counselor at an Oregon*
> *reformatory school who "went all out to help me."*

Overall, the thing to remember throughout a crisis, is that for the kid who is in it, the feeling is that he has experienced the straw that broke the camel's back. What the helper is attempting to do is to understand the feelings associated with the straw that broke the camel's back and create a way in which that load can be reduced or lightened. The Chinese word for crisis consists of two symbols: one which means danger and the other which means opportunity. So while there is an initial rise in tension associated with having failed at coping, this very tension, like the tightly drawn string of a bow, is the driving force behind the person's willingness to respond to analogies that offer new ways of coping.

When the kid agrees to creatively search for a first step, he immediately changes the dynamics of his crisis. While the kid may be still acting oppositional on the surface, often he is in the process of making the first step in his mind, his interior world, where the really important things are happening for him anyhow. *This is like the experience of the sailor who while he is fighting the wind may not know that the tide has already turned in his favor.* To tell the kid about the opportunity that lies in the danger of a crisis, the helper may say:

> *Most every child who has toasted plastic forks and knives over the campfire knows that they only change shape when they are still hot--perhaps too hot to touch. They are the most malleable when they are the most dangerous to touch.*

For more specific crisis intervention strategies and techniques consult the "Appendix" in this book. The appendix includes a discussion of some of the strategies that skilled practitioners use to intervene psychotherapeutically in crises. Below are examples of some key analogies for doing crisis intervention.

KEY ANALOGIES FOR CRISIS INTERVENTION

"The Emperor's New Clothes"
by Hans Christian. Andersen

Problem: Pretense

Hans Christian Andersen tells a fairy tale about an Emperor who loved new clothes so much that he was willing to pay any amount of money for them. One day a couple of swindlers came to his palace and offered to make him an incredible set of clothes that only wise men would be able to see. The Emperor felt that with these he would be able to distinguish the wise men in his kingdom from the stupid men. The swindlers required much gold thread and money in order to do their weaving. However, they were not really weaving. In fact, their looms were completely empty, but everyone the Emperor sent to check the looms reported that the cloth was beautiful because no one wanted to be thought stupid. Finally even the Emperor agreed that the clothes were beautiful as he certainly didn't want anyone to think that he was a fool. When he wore the clothes in a procession, all the people of the kingdom, having heard the story, exclaimed that the Emperor's clothes were beautiful. Finally, a young boy ran out in front of the parade and exclaimed that the emperor had no clothes on. Then others around agreed, realizing that they were really being dumb to buy into the ridiculous pretense. The Emperor realized he'd been had but he kept up a good front.

DISCUSSION: Can you get away with pretense forever?

* * * * * *

Digging Ditches

Problem: Procrastination

A dear friend of mine didn't want to pay for a long series of ditches to be dug alongside his road that comes way down out of the mountains for miles. Without

ditches alongside the mountain road, the spring rains would wash away the road and he would have no way to get to his house. So he solved the problem by spading out by hand a small rut along each side of the road. The rains then worked for him, deepening his ditches. The solution was simple but made all the difference in the world because it meant that he could get to his house.
DISCUSSION: How important is it to take a small step to begin?

* * * * * *

Hired Help
Problem: **Determined to refuse help**
Many times a person who is unable to get a job done around his house is amazed to find that when he hires someone to come to his house, the chore gets done. In fact, in many cases, the people themselves become major helpers to the hired person.
DISCUSSION: What is it about involving others that helps get us going?

* * * * * *

Moose Hunting
Problem: **Aggression with those you want for friends**
You don't lure a moose closer by firing a rifle. That will only drive him deeper into the forest. If you want to lure a moose, you must use a moose mating call. But if you don't get it quite right, watch out! You may find an angry moose charging you, a moose who thinks he has just been issued a challenge to fight. It takes time and practice to learn the specific calls you need.
DISCUSSION: Is the kind of message you are giving out going to attract those you are hoping to get along with? Could it be that the message that reaches others is not exactly what you intended?

* * * * * *

Trojan Horse
Problem: The Situation Is Hopeless

In the Trojan War the Greeks from Athens had been entirely unsuccessful in overrunning the fortress of the Trojans on the West coast of what is now Turkey. But as a parting gesture, they built a large wooden horse which the Trojans pulled into their fortress after the Greek ships set sail. At night the Greeks who were hiding inside the horse jumped out and overthrew the fortress.

DISCUSSION: Are things ever really hopeless or just in need of a creative solution?

* * * * * *

Call to Dinner
Problem: Selective Hearing

When my older son was little his room was so far from the kitchen that he had trouble hearing us yell "Time to come down for dinner!" Strangely enough, though, a very softly spoken mention of "chocolate chip cookies" brought him bounding down the stairs.

DISCUSSION: What's the connection?

* * * * * *

The Value of Life
Problem: Is Life Worth Living?

I once knew a man who told me that he had been questioning the value of living. Then one day driving home in a small VW thinking about how easy it would be to just give it all up, a large truck jumped the neutral ground out of control and headed straight for him. He just barely managed to swerve out of the way because there was a piece of open space on the side of the road. After stopping his car, he had to just sit there for about thirty minutes until he stopped shaking. During this time, it became very clear to him how dear life was.

DISCUSSION: Do you need to almost kill yourself to find out how dear life is?

* * * * * *

The Indian Mother
Problem: **Things Are Unfair**

Imagine how unfair you would think it to be if you were an Indian baby crying for food and, instead of saying a word, your mother covered your mouth with her hand so that you couldn't make a sound and, in fact, could barely breathe. How could you know that she had just saved you both from drawing the attention of a passing wolf?

DISCUSSION: Is it possible that things have to be unfair sometimes for good reason? Is it always possible to explain?

* * * * * *

Jumping Rope
Problem: **Unable to Relate to Others**

To jump rope when others are turning the rope, you must enter their rhythm. In fact that's why kids often accompany this game with a sing-song rhyme they chant together.

DISCUSSION: Does relating to others mainly have to do with you or the others?

* * * * * *

Playing Happily Together
Problem: **Creative Problem solving**

Five year old Jimmy was a creative problem solver. He and his friends had built a shaky block and board "house", and they were choosing roles (mother, father, etc) to play house. Robbie, an unruly 3 year old who would have knocked down everything asked if he could play. "Sure," said Jimmy after a couple of seconds pause. "You

125

can be the family dog and stand outside and guard the house." Robbie was proud and happy to have such an important role.

CONCLUSION

A kid's solutions to his problems often leads to greater problems. Any situation can provoke a crisis because a crisis refers to the kid's emotional reaction, not to the threatening event itself. The first step to helping a kid to exit the stressed out state of mind is to help him see that he needs to give up the notion that he must constantly, under all conditions, be in control. The more troubled a kid is the more he is likely to believe that, if he attempts to relax or let go of any beliefs, things will really fall apart.

Analogies can give a kid a grip on something to encourage him to believe that he can control himself adequately without trying to tightly control all the events around him. At the fair, if you don't get dizzy, the whirly rides are fun, but if you get dizzy, you want to stop the ride. If you could control your dizziness, you wouldn't need to control the machine. In dance class one is taught to keep one's eyes on a fixed spot as one whirls around to keep from getting dizzy. Of course you loose sight of the spot for an instant each time you turn. But it is enough to keep your eyes on it most of the time. An analogy is like the fixed spot. To keep his bearings (be in control) the kid must keep refocusing on it even if it is not in front of his eyes every second.

A major step in crisis intervention is to help the kid see that he doesn't have to find the perfect solution to life's problems. It is important to help him see that his own imagination is a powerful force in determining how he reacts in a crisis. The final step is to have the kid develop a plan, practice it with simulated crises, and evaluate how well he does.

7

SEEING THAT KIDS ARE TAUGHT WELL

*"We pass through this world but once. Few Tragedies
can be more extensive than the stunting of life, few
injustices deeper than the denial of an opportunity
to strive or even to hope, by a limit imposed from
without, but falsely identified as lying within."*
--Stephen Jay Gould

**GETTING KIDS TO SUCCEED IN SCHOOL HAS A
LOT TO DO WITH HOW THE KID IS TAUGHT.**
It is hard to overestimate the benefits that accrue to
students who learn from good teachers. In fact. teaching
is one of the most responsible and demanding of jobs, and
those who do it well are perhaps a culture's greatest
heroes. This chapter provides analogies and strategies both
for teachers and parents to use in working with kids as
well as for parents and educators to use in working with
school staffs.

School systems are bureaucracies. Like all
bureaucracies, schools operate on decision making systems
that don't necessarily play to the strengths of an
individual kid. Even if you are a school teacher, you
have to watch how your friends in the bureaucracy make
decisions about your kid to ensure that he gets the best
opportunity to learn.

A parent can use analogies with the school staff when

they are trying to make a decision about the child which the parent strongly opposes. He might say,

> *You know I find myself in the kind of situation that sometimes happens when I talk with my mechanic. I know nothing about cars, and he knows everything. Sometimes when I try to point out a problem to him, the car doesn't do it in his presence, and he looks at me wondering if I really know what I'm talking about. He's the expert on cars, but I'm the expert on the sounds and nuances of my particular car. Maybe, it's the same way with my kid at school. Educators know far more than me about instruction in general but maybe I need to be the expert on the important nuances that motivate my particular kid to learn.*

The reason for using the analogy here is not to attempt to manipulate the school staff into changing its view to that of the parent's, but to give the parent a way to communicate with the school staff that puts all concerned at greater ease when the parent decides to be assertive in decisions regarding his kid. Men of good will can agree to disagree, and analogies can help to make the process more tolerable.

ANALOGIES CAN MOTIVATE KIDS

Analogies told to kids about other's (real or fictional) crises and failures on the road to learning to cope can motivate kids to believe they can reach higher goals. If someone else got through despite all of his weaknesses and problems, the kid will have reason to believe he can learn well despite his situation.

For this reason I often quote for kids Einstein's famous statement about his seventh grade problems.

When I was in the seventh grade my homeroom
teacher said that he wished I would leave school.
He said, 'Your presence spoils the respect
of the class for me.' I wanted to leave school.
My poor memory for words caused me to have
difficulties that it seemed senseless for me to
overcome.

Analogies from an adult's life can be powerful sources of inspiration and motivation. **Kids will work hard to achieve in the way that significant others have achieved and in a way that will impress significant others.** As kids come to have success academically and socially, they will continue to work hard for their own intrinsic reasons.

ANALOGIES AND LEARNING PROBLEMS

James: A Case of "Learning Disabilities" and Ridicule - Teakettle Analogy

James is the classic adolescent that people imagine when the words "learning disabilities" are used. Although James has normal intelligence, at 16 years old James could only read at a fifth to sixth grade level. And his math was only slightly better. Worse, James would often hide or destroy his homework after his parents worked half the night helping him to get it done because he was afraid that it wouldn't be good enough. He had received speech therapy from a very young age, and feared embarrassment from his speech so much that he would often cut large classes. Actually his speech sounded normal to me. According to his parents he'd received a lot of ridicule in the lower grades.

James' parents sent him to me because he had started complaining about being in the special education classes in high school which he said made him seem like a "retard." Some kids at school in fact ridiculed him as a "retard." He was beginning to skip classes and leave school. At home all he did was watch television and play with younger kids.

From working with James, I came to find that he was a very pleasant, intelligent kid who enjoyed a good discussion about almost anything as long as he felt secure that he wasn't going to be asked to perform in front of a group. Also I learned that he felt, on the one hand, that the special education classes were so boring as to be "stupid," but that, the regular classes he was mainstreamed into were too difficult, and he was likely to do something embarrassing any moment.

When James cut classes sometimes I would find him at the local library or used book store. He had an insatiable desire to learn but had a terrible self concept. He said he's rather fail than "waste" his time in a special education class or make a fool of himself in a regular class. He felt damned if he did and damned if he didn't.

Moreover, James, like so many kids called "learning disabled" was not really disabled. James had a unique learning style and perhaps different neurology but definitely not malfunctioning neurology. The majority of kids I have met who were called "learning disabled" were like James, different but not disabled learners.
This is not to say that there are no kids who are neurologically impaired, and in fact I have taught such kids in a clinical reading program.

This label of "learning disabled" is often presented to families as a useful means for getting the needed help for their kid. Also, it is proposed that by explaining to a kid the nature of his problem, his anxiety is reduced and his self esteem supported because he can then attribute his learning problems to a specific cause beyond his control rather than feel dumb or guilty. However, handicapping labels can be very negative images for kids. For James it had become a stigma. While it might have ameliorated the situation to tell James that Einstein also had learning problems, the best way to have helped James with the his negative self image would have been to avoid labeling him with an image that could become negative in the first place. Must we label kids with learning problems in order to teach them appropriately?

One of the things I did with James in order to get him to persist in trying was to tell him the story about James Watt's teakettle.

James Watt used to sit in his grandmother's kitchen by the great open fireplace watching the glowing fire and an old fashioned teakettle that hung above the fire. As he watched the steam lift the lid off the teakettle, he said to himself why couldn't steam from lots of water lift heavier things or push wheels? Then when he tried to do this, men laughed and ridiculed him saying, "Ho, ho, James Watt is going to use the clouds in his grandma's teakettle to move wagons.

When I told James the story of James Watt, he loved it because he knew it was true that a famous man had succeeded despite the ridicule, though he had a tough time of it for a while. I also told James that the best revenge was success.

Often with children such as James, who have learning problems, attention has to also be given to the abuse they have received. Stereotyping, ridiculing, and physical threats can produce serious psychological damage causing feelings of inferiority, rejection and hopelessness. Many of these kids lose relationships with friends because of academic segregation. If not addressed, the problems can continue into adult life.

I had James identify potential stressors, see these approaching, and give himself the message that he could control things. Using relaxation and visual imaging, I had him close his eyes and see James Watt's teakettle and tell himself that all the steam he let off wasn't going to blow his top because he knew how to release the pressure slowly, and he also knew how to make the pressure work for him.

The James Watt analogy could not remediate James' learning problems, but it did help reduce his anxiety by giving him a strategy for approaching his problem.

Using analogies, also helped me to build a relationship

with James. Analogies were something interesting for us to talk about while we slowly built goals based on mutual trust. The more James valued our relationship, the more he was motivated to try to develop his skills. Valuing his relationship with me and believing he could succeed induced a willingness to persevere in trying to succeed in school. With the help of some great and committed teachers James succeeded in the end.

GREAT TEACHERS INSPIRE BY ANALOGY

Most of us have known teachers who wasted class time telling corny stories from their lives. On the other hand, if we were lucky, we had a great teacher who wisely and appropriately let us learn about him though offhand remarks about his life. For example, our English teacher, knowing a lot of us felt like we had too many outside activities and other class assignments to get all of his reading and writing assignments done, "let slip" that when he was in high school he went out for cross country running and used to come home in the dark of evening worn out and still having to face several hours of homework. He made the image real by talking about the shaky, rubbery feeling walking up the stairs to his room. We made the connection between his experience as a kid and ourselves. We'd imagine ourselves just like him coming home from practice in the evening. His analogy inspired many of us to make that extra effort that made all the difference.

Kids are often looking for significant other adults who share some of their aspirations but who are not their parents. When a truly great teacher becomes a significant other for a kid, magic can happen! One of the easiest ways for a teacher to become a significant other for a kid is to share a bit of himself that resonates with the feelings and experience of the kid. This can be done through analogies, images and metaphors. William is a prime example of how powerful an analogy can be as a motivator to learn.

STUTTERING

William: The Most Severe Case of Stuttering - Winston Churchill Analogy

William's story makes a strong case for the helper to build a personal connection with the student and to pay keen attention to the affective state of the learner in order to encourage achievement, motivation and positive peer interaction.

William didn't utter more than one word at a time. He did, however, physically attack another student at least once a day. He was highly oppositional in the classroom, refusing to do what teachers told him. His eighth grade principal stated that William was the most disturbed and difficult student to teach that she had ever seen.

I began by meeting William and asking him to write down the one wish he would have if a wizard came by with a magic wand and granted him one wish. He said he wished he could stop stuttering. I then told him that, while I couldn't assure him that his stuttering would stop completely, that in very short order it could be much better if he simply followed orders. His eyes lit up. I **told him to close his eyes and I would tell him a story about a very famous man named Winston Churchill.**

I told him that Winston had saved the English people by inspiring them to fight the Nazis even though at one moment in the war it seemed almost hopeless, and that, furthermore, Winston Churchill had problems with stuttering.

I told him how, when Winston Churchill was an adolescent, he developed a mannerism called a starter to prevent his vocal cords from locking and so causing him to stutter. I then went on to tell the great war story which Winston Churchill called "England's Finest Hour." And I led up to the great speech in which Winston rallied the nation when they were nearly beaten by saying, "MmmmmmmmmmmEngland will never surrender!"

William wanted to practice Winston's technique.

After three months of speech therapy, William was able to make complex statements about his thoughts and feelings, and, though he still stuttered, he had stopped fighting his peers altogether.   Today, I still see William around town, and to my knowledge he has never spent five minutes in jail. The key to his success in ceasing to be aggressive, was motivation built on a personal relationship and a renewed sense of wonder evoked by the story of Winston Churchill.

Below are a number of analogies which I have found useful in educational contexts. Some of these analogies were given to me by teachers who had found the analogy useful in the classroom. Where I know the teacher's name, I have given the teacher credit for the analogy although in some cases the analogy came from another primary source that neither I nor the teacher can identify at this time.

ANALOGIES FOR EDUCATION

1. STUDENT DISCREDITS HIMSELF

Crawling, Walking, Reading

Student Says: "I can't do it."

Remember how difficult it was when you first tried to walk. You can't even remember how difficult it was to crawl. It seems like something you just do from the time you are born. But you actually had to learn how, and the same with walking. You do it effortlessly now; but, for a long time, you stumbled around and needed a lot of help. And riding a bike is a very difficult problem until you learn how to do it, and now you can't forget it. And reading and school studies are just the same. They're difficult at first, but later there is nothing to it. And I'm sure with this new task, the same will be true. A lot of pain at first, then it is so easy, it seems natural.

* * * * * *

"Magical Cursive"

I remember thinking that I could learn to read print. But when I watched my mother writing long hand, I figured I'd never be able to do that. It seemed like magic.

* * * * * *

2. STUDENT KNOWS ALL HE NEEDS

The Picnic Area by Ned Kerns

Student Says: "I know all I need to know."

I know a woods where there is a little dirt road that goes from the main road to a little pond. There is a picnic table near the little pond. It is really a pleasant place. But there is also a car turn around; because, once you get there, you can't go anywhere else without returning to the main road. It's a nice pleasant dead end.

* * * * * *

3. STUDENT QUESTIONS WHY HE SHOULD CONTINUE

For Want of a Nail by Ben Franklin

Student Says: "Why learn every last step," or "Why continue in school?"

Let me tell you a little saying that Ben Franklin had. For want of a nail the shoe was lost. For want of a shoe the horse was lost. For want of a horse the race was lost. Can you relate that to continuing in school and doing your work? A student once said to me that the nail is going to school; the shoe is getting an education; the horse is a good job; and the race is life.

* * * * * *

4. STUDENT WANTS ATTENTION

Ping Pong Balls by Kay Dickman

Student: Wants constant attention.

You know, in a little neighborhood lived a woman who seemed to be able to do anything. Nothing was too hard for this determined lady. One of her skeptical neighbors wanted to find something that the woman would not be able to do. After he came up with an idea, he went to the woman's house and took with him 32 ping pong balls. He told the woman that he knew she couldn't keep all 32 balls under water at the same time. The man dropped 31 balls into the sink filling it with water. Slowly the woman gathered up the ping pong balls under her spread hands. With her fingers kept together and hands held close, she could barely hold all the balls down. Just when she thought she had accomplished this feat, the man dropped the 32nd ball into the water. As it bobbed up and down, the lady tried in vain to move her hands close to the bobbing ball. If she reached out to get the one ping pong ball, she knew she could lose some or all of the others. So she took a chance and quickly reached for the bobbing ball and also quickly lost half of all she had gathered.

"You know", the teacher said to the girl, "sometimes you seem like that extra ping pong ball to me."

* * * * * *

5. TALKING IN CLASS

Long Distance Calls

Student Behavior: Talking while the lesson is going on.

Very quietly so that no one else could hear, the teacher whispered in the student's ear while a class assignment was under way. "You know, if you save your long distance calls until the weekend, the rates are much cheaper."

6. CHEATING

Strength Training

Student Behavior: Copying another student's paper.
What if you tried to strengthen your muscles by having someone help you lift weights? Strengthen your brain the same way you would strengthen your muscles.

* * * * * *

7. PERFECTONISTIC

The Huddle

Student Says: "I have to get it just right."
Student Behavior: The student perseverates and doesn't get the work done on time.
Football teams huddle after each play to decide which play to run next. They have standard plays which they all know by a number, so that all the quarterback has to say is some number like play 36. Of course play 36 is always run the same and doesn't allow for much variation. When I played football we had a guy named Larry who couldn't resist trying to change the plays slightly in the huddle to try to make them perfect. He'd always say, "If we'd just change the play a little bit, we could make a touchdown. By the time he got through telling all of us what we had to change, we'd hear a whistle. Then we'd all look up and see the referee picking up the football and moving it five yards backwards. We'd taken too much time in the huddle. I'd always say to myself, Larry's messed us up again trying to be perfect.

* * * * * *

8. IDEAS REJECTED

Sandcastles Can Be Real by Bernadette Emerson

Student Says: "Everyone says my ideas are weird."

Last summer when I was on the beach, a child was busy building a beautiful, elaborate castle in the sand. He worked for hours on that fortress. When he was finished, he ran over to a group of his peers and asked them to come over to view his work of art. In the meantime, however, a gigantic wave swept past the shoreline and washed the castle into the ocean. When the boys arrived upon the scene, the castle was gone; and they made fun of him, calling him a liar and a dreamer. A man who had been observing this from nearby approached the boy and said, "Don't be discouraged. Don't ever give up building beautiful dreams. Sometimes they may be taken away from you, and people may not believe in you or your ideas; but I saw your sandcastle."

* * * * * *

9. UNPREPARED

Fishing Without Bait by John Zink

Student Says: "I just forget."

A young boy was interested in fishing and was anxious to impress his friends with his fishing prowess. He spent all his spare time at the pond. However, most of the time he had to fish without bait on the hook because he forgot to dig for worms. Do you think he caught lots of fish?

* * * * * *

10. Being Creative

Go With Your Idea by Rick Culbertson

Student Says: "It'll look dumb."
When a child is born, he is helpless and must be carried. But, he does not stop there. He pulls himself up, takes off from anywhere. Bruised, battered, and frustrated, he keeps trying to make his way around to explore everywhere and everything. Imagine being afraid to move from the crib. How dumb would that look?

*　*　*　*　*　*

11. STUDY HABITS

Position at the Dike by Janet Owens

Student Says: "I work hard in school but I never get good grades."
Imagine you are walking by a dike and notice a large puddle of water on the ground in front of you. You see a finger sticking through a hole in the dike wall. Puzzled, you soon see the finger pulled back out of the hole; and water begins rushing out of the hole onto the ground. The finger belongs to a guy who is emerging from under the water on the other side of the dike. Clinging to the wall, he takes a large gulp of air and goes back under the water. His finger once again plugs the hole. What could you tell him about his approach to make his job easier for him?
What does the guy who studies hard but makes low grades need to do?

*　*　*　*　*　*

12. ATTITUDE

Two Brothers by Pete Marinello

Student Says: "What's the point of all this stuff you're putting me through?"

Once there were two boys,identical twins who were excited about visiting their uncle's farm. They had never visited a farm before and were filled with great anticipation of what they might discover there. Upon arriving, the first boy out of the car raced into the barn to see what there was. He looked into a stall just inside the door and saw nothing but a great deal of manure. He was tremendously disappointed and lost much of his enthusiasm for the visit. The second boy, arriving shortly after his brother, took a look in the same stall. His eyes widened and a smile appeared on his face. Seeing all the manure there, he yelled, "There must be a pony in here somewhere!"

* * * * * *

13. HANDLING UNFAIRNESS

The Closed Store by Jack Shockey

Student Says: "You don't treat me the way other people do."

Maybe I have higher expectations for you. Did you ever hear the story of the man who complained to the manager of a grocery store that the price of milk was too high at $1.89 a half gallon? "The store down the street", he said, "only charged $1.69." "Then why don't you buy your milk there," replied the manager. "They don't stay open as late as you do," said the man. "Well, we only charge $1.49 when we're closed," the manager said.

* * * * * *

14. BEING ASSERTIVE

The Parachute Jump

Student Says: "He told me to do it."
If someone you really admired jumped out of a plane without a parachute and asked you to follow, what would you do?

* * * * * *

15. BEING PERSISTENT

Keep on Trying

Student says: "I fail at everything."
You know, that has happened to a lot of great men including Abraham Lincoln. In fact, Lincoln lost most of the elections he ran in but kept on believing in himself and trying till be became the President of the United States of America.

* * * * * *

16. SAVING A FRIENDSHIP

Patch It Up by Cheryl Muldoon

Student Says: "I'll never talk to her again."
Would you throw away your favorite piece of clothing just because the clothing got a small tear in it? Or would you patch it up? Wouldn't you at least do the same for a friendship as for a piece of clothing?

* * * * * *

17. PRIDE

The Oak and The Reed

Student Says: "I'm not changing."
When a hurricane force wind slams into the coast, do you think the oak tree or the reed handles it the best?

* * * * * *

18. MAIN STREAMING/ BECOMING MORE INDEPENDENT

Sam the Caterpillar by Sally Smith

Student Says: "I don't want to leave where I am. It feels good here, and everybody will make fun of me if I go back to the regular class. I used to fight everybody and be a problem."
Let me tell you the story of Sam the caterpillar.
Nobody liked Sam because he went around eating leaves all the time and ruining plants. So, Sam went away to hide by himself for a long time. He spun a cocoon so he could be alone and protected from everything. When Sam finally came out of his cocoon, he was a beautiful butterfly and everyone loved him and treated him differently.

* * * * * *

19. "SCHOOL PHOBIA" ANXIETY

Long Distance Runner by Guy Hoffer

Student says: "I can't go to school. It makes me too uptight. Just let me stay at home until I work this out and then I'll go back to school."
Long distance runners always get pains in the side

sooner or later. At first, most of them stop and try to walk it off or just double up and hold their side. Eventually, good runners learn that the best way to handle the pain is to just keep running and after a while it just goes away.

CONCLUSION

Inspiration and motivation are the keys to engaging kids in any learning task. Analogies can serve to inspire and motivate kids. Analogies are particularly useful in teaching because the analogy can be geared to the developmental level of the kid however concrete or abstract his thinking style might be. Although giving a kid an analogy may seem like handing him a solution, actually the kid will have to go through the process of extracting the essentials from the analogy to construct a concept that he can apply to his own situation. This process of analogical thinking is a form of inductive reasoning that has long been recognized as the central component of practical intelligence. The process is truly a creative educational experience because the kid can develop and embellish the analogy.

8

SOLVING SPECIAL PROBLEMS

"One who would do good to another must do it in minute particulars. General good is the plea of the scoundrel, hypocrite and flatterer".
William Blake

This chapter provides analogies for addressing what have come to called the powder keg issues of adolescence. The analogies for addressing these issues are presented cookbook fashion. They must of course be adapted to the individual kid's needs. When I first began working with adolescents, I learned the importance of having some cookbook recipes as a place to start. These analogies are models, not cure-all remedies. They are a way to begin a personal discussion with a kid.

The first of these issues, identity, is presented in detail because it is one of the most important and most universal of of the tasks of development that an adolescent faces. Seeing an analogy used in detail with the issue of identity will serve as a model for using other analogies in other situations. Notice how the analogy helps to make the kid stop and think about what she is doing to herself. The use of analogy is a powerful tool in motivating a kid to improve his perspective taking skills. Often taking a different perspective becomes the starting point of change.

IDENTITY

Kate: A Case of Confused Identity & Drug Use - Reel Life Analogy

Kate is a good case to think about before reading the rest of the suggestions in this chapter. Her experience points up the multifaceted nature of symptoms and conflicts which make every kid's situation unique. Hence, Kate serves as a warning to helpers to tread cautiously and keep a lookout for the unexpected.

Kate was very pretty, talented and intelligent. She described herself as having debilitating anxiety and depression over not knowing how to get her acting career going, and said that she had become addicted to heroin. She said that she had gotten into some criminal activity in order to finance a drug habit. Her basic difficulties were pretty clear. She could not allow herself to enjoy any of her successes. She always compared her performance with best in the business. It was a perfect prescription for failure, and she knew it, but anything short of the highest excellence didn't feel good. Drugs were a perfect out she said. On heroin, she claimed to feel comfortable doing nothing.

I began counseling by asking Kate what was the most repulsive act she could imagine. She said, "the slaughtering of calves." I then challenged her as homework to bring me examples of her own slaughtering of the joys in her life. She took the assignment very seriously. One example she related was watching a sunset from down in a valley. She remembered that the moment was beautiful until she told herself that it wasn't half as good as if she could be seeing it from the mountain top. Another example involved her relationship with a boy friend. She reasoned that, if someone was giving her a lot of attention, the person must not be the best she could do. It was like the old Groucho Marx statement. "I wouldn't want to be a member of any club that would offer me membership."

The way she communicated with herself helped to insure that she would never be happy. For example, while she wanted to be unique, she was certain there was something wrong with her for being very different in her personality from others. This was a hopeless paradoxical trap she imposed on herself. She worried about her outbursts of joy that were more intense than other people's joy, as she saw it. She felt she was like a child who could never mature. She catastrophized frequently. She said people delighted in her childish ways, but it all just went to show that she'd never make it as a woman.

This is the kind of confusion about identity, career goals, parent expectations, self-esteem needs, superwoman fantasies, and overgeneralizing and catastrophizing thought processes that added up to heroin addiction for Kate. I told Kate she was lucky to have the kind of addiction that responded to a change of living context. I told her that many soldiers had returned from Vietnam as heroin addicts but easily dropped using the drug when they came home because the context was different. She agreed that away from the big city, she didn't seem to need the drug either. But, she wanted to return to the big city to pursue her career goals, so she was worried.

I later had a discussion with Kate about "reel life" and "real life." The analogy came from a television interview with Jack Lemmon. It was perfect for Kate. She needed to distinguish between "reel life" where anything imaginable could happen and "real life": where we are highly successful if we bring a bit of the possible to fruition. The tremendous support of her family and her own commitment coupled with her strengths helped Kate make a good adjustment. The analogies between "reel life" and "real life" and the "slaughtering of joy" will be landmarks to which she will be able to return as the years tempt her to lose sight of where she is headed.

ANALOGIES FOR OTHER POWDER KEG ISSUES

DIVORCE

Important issues for kids when families are divorcing are often that of guilt, shame and security. Kids need to know they didn't cause the divorce; they can't save or restore the marriage; and that their emotional and physical needs will be taken care of. If kids enjoyed school before their parents divorced, they may see school as a sanctuary and seek support from the teaching staff (Kelly and Wallerstein, 1980).

IT'S TOUGH GOING ON AFTER DIVORCE BUT EVERYONE MUST ROW WITH THE OARS HE HAS.

SCHOOL FAILURE

Assuming the kid has a decent teacher who provides him with appropriate work, positive feedback and a classroom environment that is conducive to staying on task, school failure results from three main factors: a belief that there is no point in trying, missed homework and absences that break the continuity of study and leave the student unable to understand instruction when he returns, and emotional problems with stress and worry that takes his mind off the task at hand even if he does everything else right.

HAVE YOU HEARD OF THOMAS EDISON THE MAN WHO INVENTED THE LIGHT BULB AND FOUNDED THE FIRST INDUSTRIAL RESEARCH LABORATORY IN THE WORLD? DID YOU KNOW THAT HIS FATHER FELT HE WAS STUPID, NEIGHBORS AND FRIENDS OF THE FAMILY TOLD HIS MOTHER THAT THEY AGREED WITH THE SCHOOL THAT HE WAS MENTALLY ILL. HIS MOTHER FINALLY WITHDREW HIM FROM SCHOOL AND TAUGHT HIM HERSELF. AREN'T WE ALL THANKFUL THAT SHE DIDN'T GIVE UP ON HIM AND EVEN MORE IMPORTANTLY THAT HE DIDN'T GIVE UP ON HIMSELF! WHILE ONLY A FEW KIDS CAN BE

147

LUCKY ENOUGH TO GROW UP AND INVENT A LIGHT BULB, I KNOW THAT YOU CAN MAKE A VALUABLE CONTRIBUTION AND I AM NEVER GOING TO GIVE UP ON YOU. WHEN WE WORK ON YOUR HOMEWORK TOGETHER AND YOU'VE HAD IT, REMEMBER I'M NEVER GIVING UP ON YOU NO MATTER HOW UPSET WE MAY GET.

TEEN PREGNANCY

Through the broadcast media and a variety of other powerful ways sex is advertized to kids daily. Then there is peer pressure which offers acceptance based on sexual activity. Few kids discuss sexuality with their parents and arrive at the conscious decision to be or not to be sexually active. Instead, too often the issue of sexual activity is too anxiety producing to discuss. Sometimes parents just let their expectations be known and aggressively attack the kid if they even suspect that the kid might not be living up to their expectations. The idea with girls for example is that good girls don't plan such things, but if sexual intercourse accidentally happens on a Wednesday night in her boy friend's car, then it is just some bad luck that a good girl had. We need to be clear that sexuality is not a luck issue. It is a biology issue. Many teenagers tell me that the strong impetus to their becoming sexually active was the need to "fill a void." Many girls cited the lack of any male companionship except through boyfriends as a motivator for early sexual activity. Keeping communication open, providing good information on prevention and/or contraception and creating a feeling in the kid that he is truly trusted and will be accepted no matter what happens are probably the best way to deal with adolescent sexuality.

WHEN PIONEERS OR EXPLORERS SET OUT ON A JOURNEY, IS IT BEST FOR THEM TO GO AHEAD AND HAVE CHILDREN OR TO WAIT UNTIL THEY ARE SETTLED? DID ALL PIONEERS SUCCEED IN NOT HAVING BABIES BEFORE THEY WERE SETTLED? IS

WISHFUL THINKING THE BEST WAY FOR BRIGHT PEOPLE TO ENSURE THAT THINGS HAPPEN THE WAY THEY WANT THEM TO HAPPEN?

SUBSTANCE ABUSE

Kids abuse substances for many reasons, but in almost all cases the kid initially denies that he has a problem. Often the family back him in this denial because they honestly aren't aware of their kid's problem and are sure they know their kid. Often the kid abuses substances to gain peer acceptance and the need is more important than any reason the parents can offer for not abusing substances. If the family fails in their efforts to take him away from his substance abusing peers, then I suggest that one of the parents obtain a leave of absence from work and take the kid off on a camping trip or at least get away from the local environment to a place where the kid and parent are likely to be able to spend some quality time together. Camping is good because it's hard to find substances to abuse in the woods, and if you trek in deep enough it's hard to walk out. If taking extended leave without pay from work sounds expensive, try paying the price of a residential institution or the price of a kid hooked on drugs for life. Analogies need to focus on getting the kid to be aware of the seriousness of his problem.

YOU KNOW SOMETIMES I FEEL LIKE THE MAN WHO BOUGHT A TALENTED ANIMAL THAT HE HAD WATCHED WORKING DILIGENTLY AND COOPERATIVELY. ONLY TO BE UNABLE TO GET THE ANIMAL TO DO ANYTHING. WHEN THE NEW OWNER WENT COMPLAINING, THE OLD OWNER SAID THE ANIMAL WAS FINE, "I JUST GOT HIS ATTENTION BY SLAMMING HIM IN THE HEAD WITH A BOARD. "WHAT I AM GETTING READY TO DO MIGHT SEEM TO YOU LIKE I'M SLAMMING YOU IN THE HEAD WITH A BOARD BUT I TRYING TO PREVENT YOU FROM DESTROYING YOURSELF."

REBELLIOUSNESS

Rebelliousness is almost certain to be a problem when families are either overly controlling, overly protective or overly detached. But rebelliousness is also a part of growing up. It is important not to mistake a kid's normal task of separating from the family as a serious problem of rebellion and by focusing on it make it a negative mode of communication in the family. Analogies need to focus on the regaining of positive communication.

WE SEEM TO BE LIKE FLIES CAUGHT IN A SPIDER'S WEB. THE MORE WE STRUGGLE TO TALK FREELY WITH ONE ANOTHER THE MORE WE BECOME TANGLED UP.

ITS TRUE YOU HAVE A RIGHT TO BE HEARD, BUT YOU CAN'T SOLVE PROBLEMS WITH YOUR RIGHTS. SOMETIMES WHEN I'M DRIVING , A BIG TRACTOR TRAILER BEARS DOWN ON ME AND I KNOW I'M RIGHT, BUT I ALSO GET OUT OF HIS WAY

LOSS AND GRIEF

Of course loss and grieving is not unique to kids. However adolescents tend to magnify everything that is painful. I've seen kids become very aggressive because they equated their loss with the world treating them unfairly.. Loss for a kid does not necessarily mean a death. Significant loss for a kid can just as easily result from divorce, break up with a friend, moving to another location or simply loss of a state of mind or way of feeling. Sometimes kids react to loss with feelings of guilt. In the case of a significant other who has died, guilt reactions can be dangerous because they can lead to the decision to die. One thing helpful to kids is to have a ritual for dealing with loss which sanctions the kid's right to feel sad. Unfortunately kids don't have many places to retell their stories. So it is helpful to let a kid talk about his loss as much as he needs. It can be helpful to know that grief is not something that goes away quickly. Often grief is a life long experience. It can return at any time throughout life. One very helpful act is to ask kids to find an appropriate and positive way to keep the memory of the object of loss alive and positive. With kids whose grieving causing them to react aggressively, you might say,

YOU ACT TOUGH BUT YOU KNOW THAT WHILE A PERSON IS LIVING HE IS SOFT AND TENDER. HE BECOMES HARD AND TOUGH WHEN HE IS DEAD.

LONELINESS/WITHDRAWAL

Loneliness and withdrawal like the other paths kids sometimes take can be very different experiences to different kids. Still I often speak to a kid who is lonely but says he just doesn't want anyone and it doesn't sound too different from the kid who being very depressed withdraws and says he doesn't need anyone. Webster's attempts to define the difference between the two on the basis of control. The lonely one is rejected while the withdrawn one rejects others. I always go on the assumption that most kids would rather be experiencing a meaningful relationship with at least one other kid no matter what the kid says, and so I use analogies in the beginning that address the need for others in an attempt to get the kid motivated to be honest with himself and seek what he wants.

HAVE YOU BEEN WONDERING WHY YOU FEEL SO LONELY? HAVE YOU BEEN WONDERING IF OTHER KIDS ARE AS LONELY AS YOU? HAVE YOU BEEN WONDERING IF THERE ARE OTHER KIDS OUT THERE WHO WOULD LIKE TO MAKE CONTACT WITH SOMEONE LIKE YOU?

YOU KNOW THE PROBLEM WITH WITHDRAWING FROM OTHERS IS THAT WE CAN'T KISS OUR OWN LIPS. IF WE SHUT THE WINDOW TOO TIGHTLY, WE COULD DIE OF STAGNANT AIR. OPENING UP TO OTHERS CAN BE

RISKY AND PAINFUL? TAKING RISKS REQUIRES COURAGE AND HOPE WHICH WE HAVE TO BUILD UP WITHIN OURSELVES. ITS HARD TO EVER FEEL READY. I REMEMBER WANTING TO LOSE JUST A LITTLE BIT OF WEIGHT BEFORE TAKING PART IN EXERCISES FOR LOSING WEIGHT.

BULLYING

Bullying is a form of victimization. Often parents school officials and others take the view that it is an experience we all have to go through. The truth is that it is an act of violence by one kid against another. Adults should approach it in the same way they would any other type of violence. If talking things out doesn't work, then the police and/or juvenile services need to be contacted. Charges need to be filed. Parents and others should not advise children to hit back. It is better to help kids to learn how to respond both verbally and nonverbally so as to be assertive, but nonviolent. When telling a kid to walk away from the bullying and ignore it, it is also important to give kid a way to handle his feelings while he is attempting to ignore the bully.

A SCHOOL COUNSELOR NAMED ELIZABETH DEVILBISS OFFERS THE FOLLOWING SUGGESTION: HAVE THE CHILD THINK OF THE BULLY'S ACTIONS AS TRASH AND IN THE CHILD'S MIND'S EYE SHRINK THE BULLY DOWN TO THE SIZE OF A FLY WHICH MIGHT BE HOVERING AROUND THE TRASH.

CULTS

While there is nothing uniform about cults, many who join cults say they do so while depressed or confused. It is probably safe to say that a kid joins a cult to find more meaning in life. Cults offer immediate relief for the developmental crises of kids. Cults address the need to belong to a group, to date, to individuate from the family, to have an identity, to begin a career, and to make decisions about sex, marriage and philosophy of life. The cost for cult membership is often an intense degree of obedience to the rules of the cult. When a kid decides to leave a cult, he often returns to face developmental crises such as that of who he is and what he going to work at becoming. Where the cult provided ready answers for the tough developmental questions, often an emotional vacuum is left for the kid to struggle to fill. Also, there is the loss of an elite status in which the kid feels that he is on the cutting edge of the most important work in which mankind could be engaged. In my opinion, the best way to work with a kid attempting to leave a cult is to learn enough about the lore of the particular cult to be able to help the kid in a way that fits his unique experience. The kid and his cult experience need to be respected as a very intense, personal experience which can't be judged by anyone who hasn't been there. It is particularly important in this case that analogy and image be constructed with the collaboration of the kid. The helper needs to be able to help the kid cope with any combination of feelings of guilt, rejection, loss, failure, fear, manipulation, dependence or abuse. The helper needs to make a positive statement about returning from a cult.

WILLIAM BLAKE SAID THAT "THE PATH OF EXTREMES LEADS TO THE PALACE OF WISDOM." BUT I HAVE FOUND THAT IT IS USUALLY WHEN ONE HAS RETURNED FROM THE PATH OF EXTREMES AND HAS TIME FOR REFLECTION AND FOR INTEGRATING THE EXPERIENCE INTO ONE'S LIFE THAT THE GREATEST WISDOM COMES. ALDOUS HUXLEY, WHO EXPERIMENTED IN EXTREME PATHS HIMSELF, SAID THAT MANY PEOPLE CROSS THE LINE AND LEAVE ORDINARY LIFE TO SEEK ANSWERS IN THE EXTREMES, BUT THOSE SEEKERS WHO ARE TRULY CREATIVE ARE THOSE WHO DON'T FORGET TO COME BACK

9

EVOKING MYTHIC JOURNEYS

"Each one of them had his own dream,
his wish, his secret heart's desire,
and yet they all flowed together in
the great stream."
Herman Hesse

WHEN A BACKPACKER SETS OUT ON A TRIP, HE TAKES STOCK OF WHAT HE HAS IN HIS BACKPACK. HE LEAVES BEHIND WHAT HE WON'T NEED AND TRIES TO DISCOVER, AS BEST HE CAN, WHAT HE WILL NEED.THE KID WHO WANTS TO CHART A NEW COURSE FOR HIS LIFE CAN PROFIT FROM DOING THE SAME WITH HIS MENTAL BAGGAGE: TAKING STOCK OF THE IMAGES THAT FILL HIS BRAIN AND DISCOVERING NEW IMAGES HE CAN USE ON THE NEXT LEG OF HIS JOURNEY.

Guided fantasy or guided journey as it is sometimes called is a metaphorical method that can be used to help kids visualize where they are and what changes they need to make. Looked at simply, the guided journey is the process of one person telling another or group of others a story in which the images of setting, events of the plot and the descriptions of the characters are left sufficiently vague so as to enable the participant to fill in pictures of his own situation in life. The kid closes his eyes and takes an imaginary journey on which he confronts the

154

crucial tasks of development in a quiet, private, safe space within his own imagination. Often classical or new age music is used to create a mood. These journeys require time, commitment and concentration on the part of the kid. They illustrate how intensely and extensively analogy, image and metaphor may be used in addressing the developmental needs of kids.

In most cases these journeys are be led by a counselor. However, I've seen them led by drama teachers and other storytellers. The person who wishes to lead the journey should be willing and able to discuss any thoughts or feelings that may be evoked in the kid by the experience or be able to refer the kid to someone who can do so. My experience has been that kids love to lose themselves in fantasy. For a number of years I have conducted a guided journey as part of a presentation I do at a yearly seminar for juniors and seniors taking honors classes in the local high schools. The response is always very positive. Parents in search of someone who conducts guided journeys can usually obtain such information from their local school counselor.

MYTHIC JOURNEYS

I call these experiences, mythic journeys because the themes of each of the stories I use are based on myths which have been reiterated in various forms, be it fairy tales, art or religious stories, for thousands of years. As Joseph Campbell (1949) says in the *Hero With A Thousand Faces*, *"It has always been the prime function of mythology and rite to supply the symbols that carry the human spirit forward, in counteraction to those other constant human fantasies that tend to tie it back."*

A example of the fantasies that tend to tie kid's spirits back are those power fantasies of early childhood in which the child saw himself as the absolute center of the universe. Mom and Dad existed only to serve him as did all the toy stores. When he saw a movie with a hero who could take on any odds and succeed, he saw himself and believed he would be that awesome hero. While the myth of the awesome hero can be essential to helping us get by at an early stage of life when we feel powerless, such a myth becomes a great hinderance which we must give up later if we are to mature and become responsible.

It is helpful for kids to have symbols to help carry their spirits forward as they attempt to push through the passages toward greater maturity. In fact what the myths show us are amazingly similar stories from every age and culture of a proud hero in love with his own abilities venturing out to a strange place to confront awesome powers, subdue them, in the process learn how fragile a being man is, gain wisdom and return to share it with his comrades back home.

In what is perhaps the oldest story known to man, the Mesopotamian Pre-Biblical story of *Gilgamesh,* man is shown taking the mythic journey that becomes standard in literature throughout the world. The hero, Gilgamesh, the king of the Summerian city of Erech, leaves home, is initiated into the mysteries of the outside world and returns a more mature member of his tribe. He first ventures forth to over power the strongest of other men, Enkidu, and become his friend. Together they slay the most powerful of monsters, and they celebrate, but later Gilgamesh must mourn the death of his friend, Enkidu. Gilgamesh then sets out alone on a journey to find the secret to living forever. The secret turns out to be a plant which he recovers from the bottom of the bottomless sea. Then, while Gilgamesh sleeps, a serpent steals the plant, eats it and becomes young. Gilgamesh returns to his home saddened by the loss of immortality which he would have given to his people. He questions the meaning of life. It is the one of the oldest pieces of literature and yet one feels it could have been written yesterday.

Gilgamesh models the rites of passage through life which all kids face. He needs to develop a strong self concept, separate from his family; individuate in part through interpersonal relations with his peers; develop empathy and compassion from both celebrating and crying with valued friends over encounters with the threats that life presents; achieve good works and then face giving up all achievement and even life itself while keeping one's integrity and a sense of meaning. Whether we look to fairy tales or existential novels we will find the hero experiencing a series of transformations similar to that of Gilgamesh.

What looks on the surface to be our own personal, accidental, unique journey, turns out to be a variation on an ancient journey common to all men. Myth can prepare kids for the road ahead. Mythic journeys using guided imagery can give a kid the opportunity to practice successful transformations he needs to make in order to mature.

CROSSING THE THRESHOLD OF MATURITY

That kids experience crisis and struggle is well established. No matter how far back in history we go, we find people looking at the behavior of a certain segment the youth and making forecasts, often dismal, of what is to come. In fact, these forecasts tell us more about the men who wrote them than about the youth of the time. The youth of any time take too many forms to be pinned down and labeled. For example, when I lived in San Francisco during the 1960's as a student, I observed that there were kids living in the Haight-Ashbury district who experimented with drugs, attended all kinds of gatherings, generally took part in the happenings of the day and at the same time held down a responsible part time job, attended school, made outstanding grades, and didn't dress or act like the stereotypical hippie. Perhaps more than anything else, youth presents itself as a paradox to the older generation.

In all times youth has been a time of struggle to cross the line from being dependent on others and disciplined by others to being self disciplined, independent and responsible. At different times and in different groups of kids the struggle is approached differently and with more or less difficulty. The bottom line however is the same.

If you can't cross the threshold from dependence to mature independence, you're likely to have trouble in store.

In ancient times and today, in more primitive cultures, there are very clear cut rites to signal and guide the kid safely across the threshold from dependency to maturity. Today in our own western culture the rites of passage are much less clear. Today as always kids need guidance when they begin the task of searching for the answers to bring harmony to a changing body, changing mind, changing identity. One way of providing help to kids is to offer a mythic experience, in which kids can take their own unique journey, find their own individual solutions to the many different types of problems they run into crossing the threshold to an independent identity.

GUIDED JOURNEYS INTO THE SELF

From a child's earliest days he told stories by family, teachers, media and friends. It is not a new experience for a kid to sit and listen to and/or watch a story and then identify with a character or imagine himself a character in the story.

Guided journeys provide a structured format for enabling a kid to create images of the changes he wishes and needs to bring into being. A counselor or story teller provides an outline of a mythic journey that is open-ended allowing for the kid to fill in the unique descriptors of his own experience and yet moves with certainty to require the kid to struggle with the crises such as identity, relationships, loss, guilt, personal industry, purpose, power, autonomy, dependence and other issues central to making a good crossing from youth to maturity.

A guided journey, while it may be conducted with one kid or a room full of kids, allows the kid to sit quietly with his eyes closed, in his own space, creating his own pictures of and solutions to the situation through which he is being led by the counselor or story teller. [A word of caution to the leader of a guided fantasy is that the experience can be very powerful and may require that the kid be counseled during or following the experience.] Of course, all a kid need do is open his eyes to end the visualization, but he may be left with thoughts and feelings which have to be addressed. Anyone conducting guided fantasies should insure that all participants are very awake and mentally alert before leaving the room.

Often thematically appropriately music is used to create a mood. Lights may be adjusted. The outside world is often made more distant by choosing a site for the guided fantasy that allows for minimal intrusion by others not participating. An appropriate setting allows the participant to leave business as usual behind for a brief period and to focus solely on being creative within himself. Joseph Campbell (1988) has written himself of taking the time and finding the place to be creative within oneself as a necessity of our lives. As he says,

This is an absolute necessity for anybody today. You must have a room, or a certain hour or so a day, where you don't know what was in the newspapers that morning, you don't know who your friends are, you don't know what you owe anybody, you don't know what anybody owes to you. This is a place where you can simply experience and bring forth what you are and what you might be. This is the place of creative incubation.

SKETCHES OF GUIDED JOURNEYS

1.
ISLAND JOURNEY

A. It is a sunny day at the beach. Ocean waves are rolling in one after the other. White puffy clouds float overhead in a deep blue sky. Gulls cry and a slight breeze takes the edge off the sun's rays. You feel a warm glow as you walk along the edge. Ahead are the docks and the marina.

B. As you draw closer to the docks you see several
people in line to board a large oceangoing sailboat.
You read the sign that announces this
to be a sailing trip to an off shore island and
so you climb aboard for the trip. You are alone
and on a vacation for several weeks, so you are excited
about taking the unexpected journey.

C. On the trip across the water you watch the bow cutting
through the waves and wonder what life
is like on the island. You are happy that for
weeks you have let the old thoughts from your regular
life sink away and you can be whoever you wish.
You don't know any of the people you encounter.

D. When you arrive, you are taken to a small thatched
cottage and welcomed by a man and a woman who are
both dressed in bright clothes. They have a kind of
balloon tethered just above each shoulder.These
balloons, they say, are filled with a substance like
helium which makes walking and moving easier and
lighter. They instruct you that you are to change into
a different costume for the time you are there. You too
must wear bright clothes but the clothes can be of any
imaginable type. You can wear a sheep herder's
costume or a ship captain's attire. Today is the
beginning of a week of Mardi Gras type activities on
the island.

E. You select an outfit that you really would like
to wear if you could wear anything imaginable.

F. Then you are taken to a small theatre where you watch
a large movie screen on one wall. The lights are turned
down and you are told to watch the names being
flashed on the screen and when you find one you feel
comfortable with to take it as your new name. The
name doesn't have to make sense. It can be whatever

comes to mind.

G. You begin to walk around the island. The evening is coming on. In the center of the town, there is a large bonfire. The people are having a celebration similar to the Fourth of July. Fireworks are bursting overhead; musicians and jugglers are entertaining. There is food and games.

H. You sit down on a bench next to someone who is dressed like a wizard. He suggests that you should consider living for a while on the island. He further tells you that you can work at whatever job you would like just to see how it suits you. You tell him that you are not trained at some jobs you might be interested in, and he says that all jobs are learned by apprenticeship, and so you may choose whichever job you like and become an apprentice for a while just to see if you like it.

I. You choose a job.

J. Then you imagine the celebration ending. You go to your first day at work. See yourself walking through the entrance to where you work. See yourself beginning work. Experience the feeling of the new job. Notice your fellow workers.

K. You return home. Before going to sleep, you decide whether to stay on the island a while longer or to return to the mainland.

L. Think about the thought or feeling that you would most want to remember from this island journey so far.

M. Begin to wake up and experience the new day. Open your eyes and watch the morning sun rising over the water. Hear the gulls and surf. Feel the morning mist. Smell the ocean.

O. To the extent that you feel comfortable, pair
off with another person and discuss your journeys.

P. Consider sharing any fascinating moments with
the large group.

Q. See me if you have any personal concerns the
experience has evoked and which you feel the
need to discuss with me alone.

DISCUSSION: This journey is described in some fullness
so that the reader can have a sense of the type of patter
and commentary that creates a mood and keeps the
journey moving. This journey allows the participant to
experience change in a non-threatening manner. He goes
to a different culture with no one from his past. He takes
on new name, clothes, job, friends, house and makes
decision whether to return to old ways. **The sudden shift
in plans on the beach and the unexpected journey to
another island is similar to Ulysses journey in the
Oddessy.** The kid, like Ulysses, is thrown out of his daily
habits, and is offered the opportunity to think about
himself and his identity in an entirely different way. One
way to think about this journey is that it is an
opportunity to experience the initial separation from
family and village that the hero in myth experiences.

2.
RABBIT WARREN

A. You are exploring a big old tree with great furrowed
roots. Tucked beneath the crook of one root you find a
rabbit hole that you somehow manage to crawl into.

B. You find a labyrinth of channels.

C. A very friendly person in the labyrinth gives you a

ball of shiny cord to unwind along the way and so find your way back.

D. You take a channel which leads to a large cave where prehistoric people are huddled around a great fire. Animal figures are painted on the walls all around.

E. You can't understand their language.

F. You sit down and listen to them chanting and singing and get sucked into their rhythms.

G. They take turns dancing.

H. They gesture to you to take a turn dancing. You decide whether to do so or not.

I. You look around and survey the group to find a person who appeals to you to get to know. You sit by that person. Observe all that you can about the person. What type of person is he or she?

J. Join the group in making a mask for a ceremony of some type. Remember what your mask looks like. Take note of the type mask your friend has.

K. Begin to dance with the others who are now acting out preparation for a battle. Notice a man in a great bear skin jumps into the center of the dancing group. The men seem to know immediately what the animal represents but you are not sure. This monster animal could be their greatest fear, or their enemy, or their source of food or their guilt for past actions.

L. You decide what the beast will be for you.

M. Some men start to act out the killing of the beast and you decide whether or not to join them.

N. You eat, drink with the participants and sleep.

O. When you awake, you choose whether to go with the
others through a door that leads
to the hunt or to follow the string back
through the opening you came in.

DISCUSSION: The visit with prehistoric man can also be
a journey into a kid's own unconscious and past. As in
Alice and Wonderland, the kid is given the opportunity to
enter through a mysterious hole into another time and
place. It gives the kid an opportunity to look at
interpersonal relations on a feeling level. The kid can
pick out someone he likes without being able to speak to
him. It is an opportunity to kill whatever beast he carries
around within himself. As in the *Knights of the Round
Table*, he can become the hero who slays the monster. As
in the myth of *Theseus* the hero finds his way through
the labyrinth with the help of another. One way to think
of this journey is to see it as the stage of the hero's
journey in which he is initiated into a new stage or way
of being.

3.
ANIMAL TRANSFORMATION

A. You climb a mountain. The day is sunny.

B. You come upon a forest and enter it.

C. In the forest you find a stream.

D. You sit beside the stream with you feet in the cold
water, and the noon sun bringing a warm glow to your
face.

E. You sit still watching animals pass near by.

F. You see birds flying overhead.

G. You move into the underbrush and wait for animals

H. You.look for an animal that appeals to you.

I. When the right animal comes you face him.

J. You communicate with the animal. Talk to him about what makes him happy and sad.

K. Then you merge and become one with the animal.

L. While one with the animal you think of all the possibilities and skills of the animal.

M. Imagine what you might learn from being the animal.

N. Consider remaining the animal. Would you do it?

N. Once again become yourself, bid the animal farewell.

O. Save an important memory from the experience.

DISCUSSION: In this journey the kid can get out of himself. He can learn what the animal has to teach. He can experience a different kind of being. He can experience the unique bond between the hunter and the hunted. He may recognize his dependence upon beings weaker than himself. In ancient myth, the gods sent animals to instruct man. Some Indian tribes believed that it was animals who first had the greatest wisdom. Kids can find their totem as Indians once did. The kid's totem is an animal or plant for whom he seems to have an affinity. One way to think about this journey is to see it as a stage in which the kid takes on a special knowledge that can be his secret protection.

It is also a moment in which he must confront the fact that all beings have limitations.

4.
CATHEDRAL JOURNEY

A. You are walking along a street in the city.
The month is August. The noise and dust in the air, the
heat and the humidity all press unbearably upon you.
In the gutters and on the sidewalk there is trash.

B. You leave the honking taxis and rotting smells outside
as you enter a cathedral. Inside it is refreshingly cool
and very dark at first.

C. Then by the flickering flames of small candles you
start to notice images on the walls.

D. You walk around the cathedral studying the statues
of the saints. You feel refreshed being in a quiet,
sacred place. Study the expressions on the statues faces..
What do you see? What are your thoughts and feelings?

E. Rich colors stream through the stained glass
windows. The air has a smooth coolness.

F. A few old people are praying. You feel acceptance.
The press of the world is lifted from you.
No matter what your religion, you can
if you so choose, walk over and light a candle
for whatever reason you may have for wanting give
someone an offering from you.

G. You feel comfortable enough to walk across the heavy
stones to a small enclosed area where a
priest sits ready to listen to any thoughts and
feelings however profound or trivial that you want to
get off your mind.

H. You decide whether or not to tell him one thing
that has been heavy on your soul.

I. Then you wander out into a courtyard enclosed by high thick walls that keep out the din of the world beyond. Cloisters ring the small garden and in the center is a fountain with water dripping down.

J. You sit and close your eyes to meditate.
You feel serene. Thoughts flit across your
mind. None of them has much power to bother
you here. Enjoy letting the thoughts come and
go. From moment to moment you choose whether or not
to focus on the ringing bells or your thoughts.

K. Later you climb the bell tower and look out
across the city. You can see where a great
fire of a few days earlier burned out a
section of a neighborhood. For a brief moment images
of what it must have been like the night of the fire
jump into view only to dissolve as you broaden your
focus, look out over the whole city, the countryside
beyond, the forest beyond that.

DISCUSSION: This journey offers a kid the opportunity to deal with loss, grief, guilt, worldly pressures and self esteem. Being inside the cathedral is an opportunity for the kid to get back in touch with the spiritual side of himself. This journey may be thought of as the return home of the hero in myth. He is able to place the events of his life into perspective.
CONCLUSION: The four mythic journeys can be thought of as specific stages in the myth of the hero. First the hero journeys away from his family and way of life; then the hero is initiated into another way of being; later through an encounter he is transformed; and finally he returns home and puts the events of his life into perspective. However, all of the four mythic journeys are open-ended enough to become whatever the kid wishes to make of each.

Myths have helped man learn how to live since the earliest times. Myth grows out of the great stream into which all men's hopes, fears and dreams flow. The themes in myth are universal. Myth takes on the great questions such as identity, suffering, heroism, spiritual vision, and death. Using the framework of myth to guide a young person on a journey in which he can look inward for answers can be exciting and rewarding. As Jesus, in *Luke*, 17:21 is reported to have said, "Behold, the kingdom of God is within you." The guided journey can help kids to see the recurring myths by which they live. The guided journey can give kids, not to mention adults, the opportunity to try on a different identity. They get to challenge the myths by which they live. The kid gets to practice the transformations he must make in order to mature. This practice can be very powerful, for, the psychologists tell us, when we imagine with intensity, we experience much the same reality as if the imaginary events were actually happening.

10

COMING FULL CIRCLE

"Clay forms pots,
But the void within creates the essence of the pot.
Walls with windows and doors make the house,
But the space within them is the essence of the house."
                              Lao-tse

Gushing like a spring not knowing where it's headed, or stopped in bewilderment on the edge of the abyss is how the *I Ching*, an ancient Chinese oracle, describes the double plight of youth.   Either rushing headlong into folly or delaying to take the next developmental step are indeed double dangers kids face, and which we as parents, counselors or teachers are called upon to guide kids safely through. The *I Ching* or *Book of Changes*, as it is called, tells us that by gradually moving onward through each crisis, one guided wisely can strengthen his character. But, cautions the *I Ching*, a person needs sufficient humility in order to be receptive to wise guidance. Receptivity is the key, and no one has yet found a sure fire method for evoking it in kids.

My approach is the way of image and analogy. A great teacher of mine, Richard Wiseman, once said,

"Language is the outer fabric of the inner design--the connected language symbols testify to the relatively close-knit, confidently maintained fibers of inner being and knowing."

I believe that skillful use of language can tap into powerful sources of change in even the most unreceptive kid. For example, when a counselor called Stretch, to her office just before his court hearing on assault, and, with tears in her eyes, asked why he didn't respect himself more than to do the things he was doing, either by accident or some kind of marvelous synchronicity, she touched something important deep within this previously unreachable kid. It was a moment when something clicked between Stretch and the counselor. It brought Stretch almost instantly back into the civilized world.

RESONANT ACTION

When resonance such as that between Stretch, a deeply disturbed kid, and the counselor happens, it reminds me of nothing so much as poetry playing itself out in the real life of the kid. It can be likened to Paul Valery's description in *The Art of Poetry*:

> *Sometimes these particularly deep states of disturbance or emotion give rise to inexplicable bursts of expressive activity whose immediate effects are forms produced in the mind, rhythms, unexpected relations between hidden points in the soul which, although remote from each other until that moment, and, as it were, unconscious of each other at ordinary times, suddenly seem made to correspond as though they were parts of an agreement or of a preestablished event.*

What Valery brings to mind is an over-reaching such as I once saw on a physical level when a frail gym instructor lifted a heavy slab of concrete off of a child in an inexplicable and unexpected burst of strength. When the woman returned the next day to the site of the accident, she was unable to budge the concrete slab. In a moment of desperate emergency, she had accomplished something she couldn't normally do and probably would never do again.

A connection. In some way for Stretch, the mention of self-respect in the right context evoked an important connection, but it wasn't one that anyone could have predicted. Stretch was capable of violent and out-of-control behavior. Nevertheless, somehow in the synapses, of Stretch's brain, from hidden points in his soul, deep and remote from each other, concerns with integrity, pride, spontaneous empathy and the desire to do the right thing were pulled together and like the click of the latch opening after the one and only right key is inserted into the lock, Stretch turned in a positive direction.

A counselor mentions self-respect in the right context and turns an apparently amoral kid around. What a paradox! You could try it with the next hundred kids and get nowhere. She grabbed something essential in this kid and yet invisible to those around him. She struck a resonant chord.

It seems that synchronistically, to use Jung's word, the troubled kid and the right word found each other at the perfect time. How can you plan things like that? What do you want to call it? When I told William, the heroic story of how Winston Churchill, a stutterer, helped save the world, and William drew an analogy to his own self as a stutterer, he released in himself a powerful burst of strength for solving his problem.

I attempt to synchronize myself with the kid in order to offer an image or analogy that he will chose to use in the way that he needs in order to best help himself. It's hard to hit on the right language. When you do, you know it. It feels good. It's poetry. It's worth a lot of trial and error.

PERSONAL RESONANCE

A good example of the power of resonant action from my own life happened when I was an English teacher. I was at the time fascinated with Buckminster Fuller, who among other things designed the geodesic dome. My wife and I had built a geodesic dome with our own hands on South Mountain in Wolfsville, Maryland, We decided to go to see Buckminster Fuller speak at Catholic University, and when some students asked if they could come, I said yes without thinking. Later, I began to worry that one of the kids was likely to be bored to death with Fuller and his futuristic ideas. The kid had seemed cynical, unhappy and down on everything.

As it turned out we got there very early and Buckmister Fuller was busy setting up a stage. The kids helped set up the stage. Later they sat in the audience entranced as Fuller told beautiful analogies and stories from his life. They had helped him set up. They had shared an emotional experience. They were ready to listen. Emotion had motivated them to be receptive. ("Emotion" in fact comes from the same Latin root, movere, as "motivation.") Analogies, images and metaphors can all be used to stir emotions.

The boy I had worried about soon did a turn around at school. He no longer appeared cynical or unhappy. Numerous teachers commented on how the kid had stopped making fun of others and had stopped putting everything down. It seemed like magic but it was one of those wonderful resonant actions in which the kid experienced exactly what he needed. Fuller had a lot of trouble in school himself. In fact he had once been thrown out of school. He could be cynical but he was far more in love with the possibilities of life, and anyone who spent the least bit of time with him felt it. He became an image in which those students of mine and I could believe. I felt good being with those kids listening to Bucky.

RECONNECTING

I think that one of the reasons it feels so good to connect with kids is because we are making contact with an earlier time in our own development. We are connecting with earlier moments that were powerful for us. We get to go back with more wisdom and objectivity and get to have the experience with the kid while he is as lost as we might have been. It reminds me of the often quoted words of T.S. Elliot in the final lines of the *Four Quartets* where he speaks of entering through the "unknown, remembered gate," where "children in the apple tree" and "a condition of complete simplicity" await all of our explorations, leading us back to where we began so that we might truly "know the place for the first time."

Reconnecting is one of the great values of being a parent. We are given an opportunity to be children.

I remember a psychology professor of mine saying that when he was in elementary school, he had been selected as a child with school problems to spend the afternoon with a professor at the nearby university who wanted to help some kids because he had once had school problems. The man was Albert Einstein. Was Albert Einstein searching for an earlier connection within himself--not the cognitive memory of it but the poetry of it in the only place it could be found--the fleeting moment of resonance with elementary school children? Carl Jung said, near the end of his life, most people who came to see him were not pathological but were trying to find meaning--wanting to be connected to something.

The bottom line then in connecting with kids is to have a love of exploration, a desire to exhaust the possible options in relating to kids for a very personal individual reason, not for a high ideal. In fact, the person who, out of lofty idealism, attempts to help these kids frequently burns out before long. If, on the other hand, he genuinely uses his interactions to reflect on his own development and transformation, then he is likely to approach every new encounter with a kid with a sense of wonder and mystery. He will strive to make himself more complete.

His striving to make himself more complete will sustain him through the stresses, frustrations and disappointments that lie in his path. Kids will know intuitively that he is genuine. They will be more inclined to listen to him.

All kids I have met wanted to learn, but many of them said they didn't and refused the teaching offered them. Winston Churchill once summed up how I think these kids felt when he said,

Personally, I'm always ready to learn,
although I do not always like being taught.

Perhaps it is for this reason that the Talmud says,

The father of the child is not the one who
conceives him but the one who teaches him.

One final word about the process of connecting with kids--that word is *integrity*. Webster's defines the word *integrity* as wholeness, uprightness, soundness, honesty, virtue. Kids sense our integrity or lack of it instantly when we attempt to connect with them. **What kids are looking for are adults who have more experience and wisdom than their friends, but who continue to share many of their aspirations, and face the challenges of life with integrity.** It's a big order.

The movie *Stand and Deliver* details the true experiences of a mathematics teacher named Jamie Escalante in a most unlikely high school in Los Angeles who inspires ever increasing numbers of students to pass the Advanced Placement Test in Calculus, a very demanding task, which only two percent of high school students even attempt. It is not his skill, organization or desire to see students succeed that is the key to encouraging students to carry through on a commitment to make the study of calculus one of the highest priorities of their lives. They witness daily, and have heard from other students about this teacher's commitment to kids and learning. It's modeling commitment, personal integrity and a belief in kids through the good times as well as the bad that enables the teacher to build the powerful connection with kids. A great teacher's life becomes a powerful image for his students to believe in.

STAYING HONEST WITH OURSELVES

One of the surest ways to turn kids off is to give them the perception that they have been told a lie. It doesn't matter that the kid himself might tell a little white lie on occasion. Kids are insecure about their identity, and when they are misled by an adult they have been relying on, they can feel as if the ground beneath them is not as solid as they thought. Joseph Conrad in his great novel, *The Heart of Darkness*, describes the intense disgust evoked by lies:

> *"You know I hate, detest and can't bear a lie, not because I am straighter than the rest of us, but simply because it appalls me. There is a taint of death, a flavour of mortality in lies - which is exactly what I hate and detest in the world - what I want to forget. It makes me miserable and sick, like biting something rotten would do."*

Analogies not only offer sage counsel to kids; but, when directed toward ourselves, can help keep us honest. As we grow stronger verbally, it is all too easy to use language to simply rationalize any of our acts as being wise and honest.

Turning our analogies back on ourselves will insure that our words are not lost when we speak them to kids. As we truly look for a fresh way to make everyday language and common events come alive with meaning for ourselves, we transform ourselves in ways that directly communicate respect to kids. There is nothing so fascinating as the experience of being startled by the everyday occurrence, and feeling that one is clearly seeing it for the first time. As Martin Heidegger said of the power of everyday language.

> *Poetry proper is never merely a higher*
> *mode of everyday language. It is rather*
> *the reverse. Everyday language is a*
> *forgotten and therefore used up poem from*
> *which there barely resounds a call any longer.*

It is the magic we infuse into everyday language and events by our honest fascination with it's power to transform our lives that appeals to kids. Our words stick and resonate according to the spirit we put into them. No matter what we may say, kids hear not the words but the essence in our communication. They hear us being inclusive or exclusive of them and their problems; they hear us being genuine or fake; they hear us being honest or false; they hear us inviting or manipulating; they hear us joyfully exploring or sarcastically going along; they hear us humbly learning or arrogantly knowing; they hear us bending and adapting or standing rigid; they hear us finding love or finding hate.

Kids approach us as a work of art. They seek the indescribable wonder in us. If we truly want to communicate with them powerfully, then we must work on ourselves as we would a piece of art. Our words can only reflect the light within us.

> *"Only one who has risked the fight with the*
> *dragon and is not overcome by it wins the*
> *hoard, the treasure hard to attain. He alone*
> *has a genuine claim to self-confidence, for*
> *he has faced the dark ground of his self and*
> *thereby gained himself...He has arrived at an*
> *inner certainty which makes him capable of*
> *self-reliance.*
> *--C. G. Jung*

APPENDIX

This section is a distillation of techniques methods, and theory I have found useful in understanding and communicating with kids. In this section I only give a brief description of each strategy or theory. In fact, many creative books have been written on all the subjects in this section. I include the name of at least one prominent person whose work is identified with each strategy. I list the person's name not to imply that what I have written is a proper explanation of his ideas, but only to give you a place to go for properly learning the skill.

1.

PROBLEM SOLVING

Use a **CONSISTENT STYLE OF COMMUNICATION** when you discuss problems with the kid. Every time you help the kid to solve a problem use a similar format. This way he will have the security of being able to anticipate what you are going to say next. This will also teach the kid to work through his problems in an organized way when you are not around. A suggested format is the following:

1. "Tell me the story of what happened or is happening. This is an opportunity to listen to the kid ventilating and observe the intensity of the problem. What events in the kid's life does the kid bring up in talking about the stress he is feeling at the moment? Is the stress of the moment

related in a significant way to the other life events he may choose to relate? Active listening and confrontation techniques that avoid power struggles are key here.

2. "What were/are the specific facts of the story?"
Observe the ability of the kid to switch from emotional, feeling descriptions of the event to cognitive descriptions and explanations of the stressful event.

3. "What would be a better way for the story to end?"
Here the kid attempts to approach the problem in a positive way.

4. "How could/can you prevent repeating the same story or the stress associated with the story?"
Here the kid problem solves.

5. "Let's try creating a new story."
Here similar problems are role played. The kid may close his eyes and imagine himself in similar situations. He can attempt to see himself succeeding in a similar situation. Here it might be pointed out to the youth that visualization can sometimes be almost as good as actual practice. He can be told that a study was done with basketball free throw shooting in which one group only visualized practicing and the other group practiced physically and didn't visualize. There was no significant difference in the improvement of the two groups.

6. "Let's practice."
Set up new crisis situations and resolve them.
Practice reversing roles as a way of helping the kid to experience insight into the other person's way of perceiving the situation.

7. "How will you know if you succeeded?"
Establish criteria for success.

* * * * *

2.
DEFENSE MECHANISMS
(See Anna Freud, 1964)

1. Projection: Kids will often attribute their own thoughts, feelings and acts to someone else.The classic response is, "He did it."

2. Denial: Kids will often deny something despite the fact that numerous people testify to its existence. For example, despite the fact that the teacher witnesses the kid with his hands on a classmate, the student will say, "I never touched him."

3. Rationalization: Kids find reasons for doing what would otherwise be unacceptable. For example, they may refuse to work in class saying they don't feel well or aren't taught properly.

4. Displacement: Kids move the source of frustration from one person or place to another. For example, if the kid is frustrated and angry with his mother but is powerless to do anything about it, he may come to school and insult the teacher or grasp at the slightest thing as a reason to attack her.

5. Regression: KIds under stress may exhibit behavior characteristic of an earlier more secure time in their life. For example, the student who storms out of the school may, as a young child, have run to his room, climbed into bed and had a nap when things got to be too much.

6. Reaction formation: Kids may develop a front that is the exact opposite of how he feels. For example, not wanting to recognize the insecurity and fear he feels about himself, he may parade around as the tough, macho type.

* * * * *

3.
THEORY OF MORAL DEVELOPMENT
(See Lawrence Kohlberg(1963) and Robert Keegan)

Failure to recognize a kid's level of moral development can frustrate attempts to work with him.
If you expect a very young child to act responsibly for the betterment of society or out of respect for you, then you are going to be in for a surprise. Most very young children do things to have fun and only think about the "moral consequences" if they are caught doing something wrong. Some older children and adolescents, though they have been growing normally physically and cognitively, remain stuck at a very early level of moral development. With regards to right and wrong, they must be dealt with as if they were very young children. For example, if a kid's basic moral position is that "I only do what's right because I'm made to," you need to encourage some moral development and plan for success based on the kid's moral level. To give such a kid broad rights and responsibilities without the support of behavioral controls, is to set him up for failure. Kohlberg's stages of moral reasoning are:

1.   Obedience: Kid bases acts on physical consequences of act. "I don't want to be punished."

2.   Logical Consequences: Kid bases acts on belief that if caught, he will have to correct any trouble he has created. For example, if he breaks a window, he'll have to repair it. "I don't want to have to clean up any mess I create."

3. Status: The kid acts to gain the respect of others. He commits acts that will make him appeal to others in the area of moral choice. "What will others think?"

4.   Law and Order: The kid feels rules must be obeyed in order for society to function.

5. Social Contract: The kid believes the rights of the individual must be protected for the good of all.

6. Universal Intrinsic Principle: The kid bases his sense of justice on principles which transcend the other stages and speak to a higher morality of what is right in a specific situation.

These moral stages and their behavioral outcomes are not to be thought of as a well ordered hierarchy of stages. An adult may fancy himself highly principled yet find himself physically attacking a friend as a wave of emotion overpowers his high moral standards. I remember when William Buckly and Gore Vidal almost ended up in a fist fight on national television when the two started throwing verbal cuts at each other while they were trying to jointly cover a political event. Whatever their high standards of justice, at that moment, they were out to get each other whatever it took.

4.
THEORY OF DIFFERENT TYPES OF IRRATIONAL IDEAS

(See Albert Ellis,1977)

Ideas can cause people to become upset   or   unhappy. Three of these used frequently by kids are:

1. Others must treat me kindly or society should punish them.

2. I should get most of what I want quickly and easily and shouldn't get what I don't want.

3. I must succeed and win approval or I am worthless.

A corollary to the irrational beliefs is that "when what

I believe doesn't pan out, then things are awful, terrible or catastrophic, and I can't stand it." Practice picking out the kid's irrational beliefs quickly and pointing them out in ways acceptable to the kid.

* * * * *

5.
ACTIVE LISTENING
(See George Gazda,1973)

Be able to convey to the kid the feeling that you have heard him, genuinely understand and empathize with his feelings. Take note that helping the kid reason out a solution to his problem is a different process from conveying to the kid that you hear how he feels.

Here is a system for evaluating your responses:

The first two responses are poor from the standpoint of attempting to empathize with the feelings of the kid; the fourth response is excellent; and the third response is fine and in many cases, the best you can expect of yourself.

1. Hurtful Response: This response abuses the kid's statement of feeling. One way to do this is to act as though the feeling isn't important.

2. Avoidance or Problem Solving Response: Whether one refuses to acknowledge the feeling, or intellectualizes the feeling by problem solving, he has chosen not to deal directly with the feeling of the kid.

3. Empathetic Response: The kid has the feeling that the adult has heard his feeling statement.One rote way to accomplish this is to simply restate what the kid has said with his exact words or slightly different words. This can results in the statement so often heard by counselors which begins, "I hear you saying," and then the paraphrase of what the kid said.

4. Insightful Response: The kid not only has the feeling that his feelings have been heard but that the listener has insight about his feelings. It is difficult to do this well and, even if done well, often closes off discussion if the kid is not ready for it.

5. Parallel Response: Inquire if the kid is experiencing similar kinds of feelings to those he would feel if listening to a certain song. Or have the kid look at a picture and ask if it is anything like what the kid is feeling. In fact I suggest keeping a book of photographs and art around just for this purpose.

6.
COLLECTING AUTOMATIC THOUGHTS
(See Beck, 1976)

This can be used to enable a kid to realize that he has negative thoughts and that they he power over him. The kid is instructed to spend ten minutes to a half hour writing down the thoughts that pop into his head. Pictures and other props can be used to evoke thoughts if needed. The kid should be told that he need not share the thoughts unless he wishes, but he should go back over the writing and circle the thoughts he thinks are negative.

7.
A-B-C ANALYSIS OF STRESSFUL EVENTS
(See Ellis, 1977)

This is the basic method of Rational Emotive Therapy. In a situation which is not stressful or even related to the kid's problem, he can be taught the system and practice using it. Then he can be en-encouraged to use it when he is in a stressful situation. This is a powerful, non-intrusive way for the kid to confront himself about the irrational beliefs upon which he bases his decisions. For example, it could enable a kid to avoid a fight provoked by name calling by identifying the following:

> A= Activating Event; name calling
> B = Beliefs
> *Irrational Belief= Name caller hates kid and thinks he is worthless
> *Rational Belief= Name caller is himself using a a poor way to relate to anyone.
> C = Consequences: anger and fighting

Ellis points out that people will say that "A" causes "C". They tend to believe that the event such as name calling, pure and simple, causes the anger and fight. Actually, Ellis points out, it is the person's beliefs that causes the fight. In particular it is the irrational belief that person holds but has no hard evidence to support that causes upset feelings. If a good friend calls a kid a name, and the kid believes his friend is simply being playful, then no fight is likely to result. Susan Walen, Raymond DiGiuseppe and Richard Wessler (1980) have written a very fine nuts and bolts book on using this method called *A Practitioner's Guide to Rational Emotive Therapy*. Michael Bernard and Marie Joyce (1985) have written a fine book on the specific applications of this method to children and adolescents titled *Rational Emotive Therapy With Children And Adolescents*.

8.
LISTEN TO SELF STATEMENTS
(See Meichenbaum, 1977)

Have the kid check out the kind of statements he gives himself and practice altering the negative statements to produce more positive results.

9.
RATIONAL EMOTIVE IMAGERY
(See Maultsby, 1971)

As a way of getting rid of negative habits, imagery is used to introduce and reinforce thinking and feeling that is more rational. First the kid does an A-B-C analysis, then he relaxes, by concentrating on his breathing with eyes closed for example. After he is relaxed, he recreates the original scene, only this time he alters the picture by seeing himself thinking and acting in a rational way rather than an irrational way. At the same time, he attempts to feel better emotionally.

10.
SUBJECTIVE UNITS OF DISTURBANCE SCALE
(See Wolpe, 1969)

The kid imagines a situation of complete relaxation and gives it a zero rating on a scale of 0 to 100. Then he is asked to imagine the other end of the continuum, high anxiety, and rate it 100. He is then asked to rate his present feeling of stress as a way of putting the experience into more rational focus.

11.
COVERT MODELING
(See Rathjen & Hiniker, 1978)

The kid imagines a model, preferably one of his peers, appropriately handling a situation that would be stressful or difficult for the kid. It is helpful to have the kid imagine multiple models handling the situation appropriately rather than just one model.

12.
ASSERTIVENESS TRAINING
(See Lange, 1977)

This is a four stage process in which the person is helped to:

1) Develop a belief system that includes high regard for his rights and the rights of others.

2) Learn to discriminate between aggressive and assertive responses.

3) Cognitively restructure his dysfunctional thoughts.

4) Rehearse assertive responses for specific situations.

Elizabeth Berry has written an excellent training manual titled *Rational Assertiveness Training* (1978). It can be ordered through the Institute For Rational Living in New York City.

13.
BIBLIOTHERAPY
(See Dreyer, 1977)

Kids may be assigned high interest readings which address their problem. The readings can focus on kids who have faced and solved problems similar to their own.. Dreyer's *Book Finder* lists numerous books, giving their reading level and a synopsis. under a wide variety of headings such as Abandonment, Adoption, Aggression, Apathy, Blame, Death, Body Concept, Boy-Girl Relationships, Crime, Depression and others. Arthea Reed's *Comics To Classsics: A Parent's Guide to Books for Teens and Preteens* is a good source for helping kids find literature they will enjoy.

14.
ANGER CONTROL
(See Novaco, 1975)

PREPARATION: A good sailor gets prepared for a squall. Need to remember to take it easy. No matter how upset I may begin to get in the situation, I know that it will blow over and I'll probably have trouble remembering it in 6 months.

CONFRONTATION: I can just let down the sails and ride the big waves out. Need to remember to keep the bow pointed into the waves and watch for what's coming next. No point getting mad. I'm not jumping to conclusions. I'm looking for positives. My goal is becoming happy, healthy and wise.

SOMATIC SIGNALS: Trembling, getting tight, gritting my teeth. I can take a deep breath. I can control myself by remembering something positive that I keep on hand just for times like this. For example I can remember the warm glow on my face of the sun shinning down as I drifted lazily along in a gentle breeze. Anger destroys blood vessels and I need mine to live a long life.

COMMUNICATION: The wind may not be going where I'd like to go, and I don't need to control it. He's right from his perspective and I'm right from mine. Even if he wants me to get mad, I don't have to get mad. I can be constructive no matter how obnoxious the other person. I can let him know that I'm looking for the sun and the best way to use the wind.

ADJUSTMENT: I can't change the wind but I can adjust my sails. I can change my expectations. It always feels better to be calm than angry. I can lighten up. I can be like the reeds that bend in gale force winds. I will be proud of myself later for staying in control.

RESOLUTION: Sailing where I need to go in winds that are going another way feels very good. I did really good. I could have gotten sucked in. I could have been swamped and drowned. I got through this without being out of control angry.

15.
MEDITATION
(See Aitken, 1982)

A way to begin meditation is to count breaths. Breathe naturally. One way for a kid to control a mind full of thoughts that is rushing like a stream out of control is to focus on counting. Simply sit in a quiet place with back straight and count "one" for an inhalation and "two" for an exhalation. The kid should continue this way until he reaches ten. Then he should begin the count of ten again. If one loses count, he should simply begin again. If a particular thought keeps intruding, then he should consider the thought until it becomes boring or in some way undesirable, and then return to the comfort of the counting. He should do this for a brief time at first and slowly build up to 15 or 20 minutes twice a day. One must be certain that he does this in a safe quiet place. One must be certain that he is fully awake before going anywhere, just as one would after waking up from a nap. Though one may sometimes become drowsy, the idea is not to fall asleep but to stay perfectly and intensely conscious and aware.

REFERENCES

Achenbach, T. M. *Developmental Psychopathology.* New York: Wiley, 1982

Aitken, R. *Taking the Path of Zen.* Berkeley, California: North Point Press, 1982.

Andersen, Hans. *Fairy Tales.* New York: Weathervane Books.

Bateson, G. *Steps to an Ecology of the Mind.* New York: Ballantine Books, 1972.

Beck, A. *Cognitive Therapy and the Emotional Disorders.* International Universities Press, 1976.

Bellack, Leopold. Lectures on "Brief Psychotherapy". Cape Cod Institute. Department of Psychiatry. Albert Einstein College of Medicine, 1984.

Bernard, M. and Joyce, M. *Rational Emotive Therapy with Children and Adolescents.* New York: John Wiley and Sons, 1984.

Bernstein, Douglas and Borkovec. *Progressive Relaxation Training.* Research Press, 1973.

Berry, E. *Rational Assertiveness Training: An Instructor's Manual.* 1978.

Bettleheim, B. *The Uses of Enchantment.* New York: Vintage Books Random House, Inc. 1975.

Bettleheim, B. and Zelan, K. *On Learning to Read.* New York: Knopf, 1981.

Bogart, Gary and Isaacson, R. *Junior High School Library Catalog.* New York: H. W. Wilson & Co., 1980.

Bowen, Murray. *Family Therapy in Clinical Practice. New York*: Jason Aronson, 1978.

Bowers, Kenneth and Meichenbaum, Donald. *The Unconscious Reconsidered.* New York: J. Wiley, 1984

Campbell, J.*The Hero With a Thousand Faces.* Princeton: Bollingen, 1949.

Campbell, J. & Moyers, B. *The Power of Myth.* New York: Doubleday, 1988.

Caplan, G. *Principles of Preventive Psychiatry.* New York: Basic Books, 1964.

REFERENCES

Carlsen, Robert G. *Books and the Teenage Reader: A Guide for Teachers, Librarians,and Parents.* New York: Harper and Row, 1980.

Coles, Gerald. *The Learning Mystique.* New York: 1988.

Deal, T. & Kennedy, A. *Corporate Cultures.* New York: Addison-Wesley Publishing, 1988.

Dollard, J. & Miller, N. E. *Personality and Psychotherapy.* New York: McGraw-Hill, 1950.

Dreyer, S. *The Bookfinder--A Guide to Children's Literature.* Circle Pines, MN: American Guidance Service, an annual library sourcebook.

Ellis, Albert. *Handbook of Rational Emotive Therapy.* New York: Springer Publishing Company, 1977.

Ellis, Albert. *Humanistic Psychotherapy: The Rational Emotive Approach.* New York: Julian Press, 1973.

Ellis, Albert. *Reason and Emotion in Psychotherapy.* New York: Lyle Stuart, 1962.

Erickson, M., & Rossi. *Hypnotic Realities.* New York: Halsted Press, 1976.

Fader, D. & McNeil, E. *Hooked on Books: Program & Proof.* New York: Berkley Publishing, 1968.

Foreyt, John P. & Rathjen, Diana P. *Cognitive Behavior Therapy.* New York: Plenum Press, 1978.

Frank, A. *The Diary of A Young Girl.*

Freud, Anna. *The Ego and the Mechanisms of Defense.* New York: International Universities Press, 1966.

Gazda, G. *Human Relations Development: A Manual for Educators.* Boston: Allyn and Bacon, 1973.

Goldfried, Marvin & Davison, Gerald. *Clinical Behavior Therapy.* New York: Holt, Rinehart and Winston, 1976.

Gould, Stephen. *The Mismeasure of Man. New York:* W W. Norton & Company, 1981.

Haley, Jay. *Leaving Home: The Therapy of Disturbed Young People.* New York: McGraw-Hill, 1980.

Haley, Jay. *Probleming Solving Therapy.* New York: Harper & Row, 1976.

Haley, Jay. *Uncommon Therapy: The Psychiatric Techniques of Milton H. Erickson, M. D.* New York: W. W. Norton & Company, 1973.

Hesse, H. *The Journey To The East.* New York: Noon Day

Press, 1957.

Hoffman, Banesh. *Albert Einstein: Creator and Rebel.* New York: New American Library, 1972.

Hoffman, M.L. "Moral Development." In P.H. Mussen (Ed.) *Carmichael's Manual of Child Psychology.* London: Wiley, 1970.

Kohlberg, L. "The Development of Children's Orientations Toward a Moral Order." *Vita Humana,* 6:11-33, 1963.

Lange, A. and Jakubowski, P. *Responsible Assertive Behavior.* Champaign: Research Press, 1976.

Lawrence, D. H. *The Complete Poems of D.H. Lawrence.* New York: Viking Press, 1964.

Lazarus, A. *In The Mind's Eye: The Power of Imagery For Personal Enrichment:* New York: Guildford,1987.

Lazarus, R. *Psychological Stress and the Coping Process.* New York: McGraw-Hill, 1966.

Lichtenberg, James. "Believing When the Facts Don't Fit." *Journal of Counseling and Development,* 1984.

Lionni, L. *Treasury of Favorite Stories.* New York: Pantheon Books, 1985.

Luria, A. *The Role of Speech In The Regulation of Normal and Abnormal Behavior.* New York: 1961.

Maultsby, M. C. "Rational Emotive Imagery." *Rational Living.* (6), 24-26, 1971.

Meichenbaum, D.H. *Stress Inoculation Training.* New York: Pergamon Press, 1985.

Meichenbaum, D. H. & Goodman, J. "Training Impulsive Children to Talk to Themselves: A Means of Developing Self-Control." *Journal of Abnormal Psychology.* 77 (2), 115-126, 1971.

Minuchin S. & Fishman, C. *Family Therapy Techniques.* Cambridge, Massachusetts:Harvard University Press, 1981.

Novaco, R. *Anger Control: The Development and Evaluation of An experimental Treatment.* Lexington, Ma.: D.C.

Palazzoli, S. M., Boscolo, L., Cecchin, G., & Prata, G. "The Treatment of Children Through Brief Therapy of Their Parents." *Family Process,* 13 1974.

Palazzoli, S. M., Cecchin,G., Prata,G., & Boscolo,L.

Paradox and Counterparadox. New York:Jason,1978. Heath, 1975

Pines, M. "The Super Kids." *Psychology Today,* 1975.

Ross, L, Leppe, M., & Hubbard, M. "Perseverance in Self-Perception and Social Perception: Biased Attributional Processes in the Debriefing Paradigm."
Journal of Personality and Social Psychology, 32.

Rathjen, D. & E. and Hiniker, A. *Cognitive Behavior Therapy.* New York: Plenum Press, 1978.

Reed, A.J.S. *Comics To Classics: A Parent's Guide to Books for Teens and Preteens.* Newark: International Reading Association. 1988.

Schwartz, Martin. *Stuttering Solved.* J. B. New York: Lippincott Company, 1976.

Shamsie, S. J. "Anti-social Adolescents:Our Treatments Do Not Work--Where Do We Go From Here?"
Canadian Journal of Psychiatry, 26, 1981.

Spengler, O. *Decline of The West.* New York:Knopf,1926.

Vellutino, Frank. "Dyslexia." *Scientific American,* 3, 34-41, 1987.

Walen, S., Digiuseppe, R. & Wessler, R. *A Practitioner's Guide to Rational Emotive Therapy.* New York: Oxford University, Press, 1980.

Wallerstein, J. & Kelley, J. *Surviving the Breakup.* New York: Basic Books, 1980.

GUIDE TO ANALOGIES

The analogies presented throughout this book are here arranged by a specific problem that the analogies might be used to address. It is important to keep in mind that these analogies will almost always need to be modified to address the individual needs of the kid with whom you are communicating. Also, with slight modification, in most cases, one analogy can be altered to meet the needs of a kid with a different problem than that problem by which the analogy is indexed.

COPING\CRISIS

CULTS

DECISION MAKING

DEPRESSION

DIVORCE

DRUG ABUSE

FIGHTING

FOLLOWING RULES

FRIENDS

HELPLESS\HOPELESS
(See Depression & Giving Up)

ISOLATION
(See Withdrawn)

KNOW IT ALL

MOTIVATION

OFF TASK

PARENTING

PARENT PRESSURE

INDEX

ABOUT THE AUTHOR

After barely graduating from a Mississippi High School, Estes Lockhart entered the Marine Corps and trained at Paris Island where he learned that he was more interested in people than discipline. Following the Marine Corps, he headed out to San Francisco where he spent the 60's finding his way. After earning a B.S. and M.A. in English Literature from San Francisco State University in 1969, Estes joined the Peace Corps and taught at the Middle East Technical University in Turkey.

Back in the States, teaching high school, he became deeply involved in helping students overcome crippling learning and behavior problems which were stunting their academic and social development. Following the success of his in-school program for these students, he founded a separate public school to serve the students in grades 6-12 needing a highly individualized alternative program. This school, currently called the Heather Ridge School, is in its twelveth year of serving the 25,000 students in Frederick County, Md. It has received wide recognition and has been the model for alternative programs in other school systems. To complement this school, Dr. Lockhart founded and directs the School Support Program, a K-12 crisis intervention program which for 10 years has helped high risk students cope socially and academically without leaving their home school.

Along the way Estes earned an M.S. in School Counseling from Johns Hopkins University, became certified as a Maryland Department of Education School Psychologist, and earned an Ed.D. from Nova University.

Today Estes lives with his wife and two sons in Frederick, Maryland where he supervises the Frederick County Public School Counseling Program and practices clinical mental health counseling. He teaches in the graduate education program at Western Maryland College, and is a frequent speaker on how to communicate with kids. When he is not busy trying to learn how to communicate with his own kids, and wife, he enjoys sailing, camping and traveling with them.

UNDERCURRENTS PRESS
BOX 384-A
FREDERICK, MD. 21701

Please send me the items I have checked.

_____*FOUR MYTHIC JOURNEYS I* (Audio Cassette).
The author of *Communicating With Kids* reads
four guided journeys: Island Journey, Rabbit
Warren, Animal Transformation and Cathederal
Journey. $12.00.

_____*WILL.* (Audio Cassette) A recreation of an
actual session with a 14 year old boy and his
mother around isssues of aggression and chronic
nonattendance at school conducted by the author
of *Communicating With Kids* which illustrates
the practical use of the forgotten language. $15.00.

_____*COMMUNICATING WITH KIDS: A PRACTICAL
GUIDE TO THE FORGOTTEN LANGUAGE.*
Additional paperback edition: $16.95.
Hardcover edition: $21.95

Please send me the Undercurrents Press items I have
checked above. I am enclosing $_____ (please
add $2.00 for postage) Send check or money order - no
cash or c.o.d.'s.

Name_____

Address_____

City_____

State_____Zip Code_____